Born Amish

Ruth Irene Garrett
and
Deborah Morse-Kahn

TURNER PUBLISHING COMPANY
Paducah, Kentucky

visit us at **ruthirenegarrett.com** and **www.regionalresearch.net**

Turner®
PUBLISHING COMPANY

TURNER PUBLISHING COMPANY
Publishers of America's History
412 Broadway • P.O. Box 3101
Paducah, KY 42002-3101
270-443-0121

Published by:
Birchem Management Inc.
Leon, Iowa
in conjunction with
Turner Publishing Inc.
All rights reserved.

Publishing Consultant: Douglas W. Sikes   Cover Concept: Ottie A. Garrett, Jr.

Designed by: Steward&Wise   Book layout: Elizabeth B. Sikes
GRAPHIC DESIGN

All material in this book is entirely the responsibility of the co-authors and is true to their research and experience. Descriptions of places and events found in this book are real in time, and are specific to the nature and the geography of the Amish communities they know best. Any similarity to individuals living or dead not actually named in this book is entirely coincidental.

Library of Congress Control No.: 2004102813
ISBN:1-56311-963-3
First Printing: 2004 A.D.
Printed in the United States of America

Contents

Other Books by the Authors:

Ruth Irene Garrett (with Rick Farrant)
Crossing Over: One Woman's Escape From Amish Life
HarperSanFrancisco, 2003 [2001].

Ruth Irene Garrett and Ottie Garrett
www.ruthirenegarrett.com
My Amish Heritage: The Pictorial Journey of Ruth Irene Garrett
Turner Publishing Company, 2003

Deborah Morse-Kahn
www.regionalresearch.net

Edina: Chapters in the City History
City of Edina, Minnesota, 1998

A Guide to the Archaeology Parks of the Upper Midwest
Roberts Rinehart, 2003

Clinton, Iowa: Railroad Town
Clinton County Historical Society, 2003

A Guide to the Amish of the Bluff Country: Iowa, Minnesota & Wisconsin. Prairie Smoke Press, 2004

Dedication

For my mother, Martha Miller, whose love is the wind beneath my wings, and to all mothers and daughters.

Ruth Irene Garrett
Glasgow, KY

For my father, Howard Kahn, who fostered my enduring respect and appreciation for the cultures and beliefs of all the world's peoples.

Deborah Morse-Kahn
Minneapolis MN

Acknowledgments

Irene:

All my love to Ottie, and to our families, and to my co-author Deborah. Love and thanks go to all our friends: in Kentucky, James and Starlot Pierce, Mark and Katherine Tooley, Don and Betty Gumm, and our family in Christ at Holy Trinity Lutheran Church; in Missouri, the Doug Sikes family; in Iowa, Ruth Reed, the ladies of the book club, and everyone at Madison Square Assisted Living in Winterset; to our "English" Amish bonnet models, Mica Pendley and Emily Sikes.

Deborah:

Blessings all around to dear Irene and Ottie, it has been only joy. Much love to all the Kahns and Ramlidens. Love and thanks go to my dear friends who looked after me so well during the writing of this book: in Minnesota, Anna Schroder, Faye Ackeret and Charlie Bailey; in Iowa, Joe Trnka.

Our sincere appreciation is also extended to those kind and thoughtful individuals who advised and supported us through the writing of this book:

To Stan and Pat Birchem of Leon, Iowa, who made this dream come true. To everyone at Turner Publishing for outstanding assistance. To Bishop Ray and Mrs. Mary Schrock of Blair, Wisconsin who knew what this effort would mean.

Last, but never least, our praise and thanks to God: for guidance, love, and the blessings that make all things possible.

Ruth Irene Garrett, Glasgow, Kentucky
Deborah Morse-Kahn, Minneapolis, Minnesota

Preface

I first met Irene and Ottie Garrett eight years ago when researching Amish life in the United States.

Ottie had authored a guidebook to national Amish communities and I had found a copy of this fascinating title on the library shelf. Not content to admire from afar, I wrote to Ottie at the publishing house address, got a delightful reply, and made fast friends of Ottie and his new bride, Ruth Irene Miller, lately out of the Amish community at Kalona, Iowa.

These many years later I watch my beloved friends move through 'English' society together. It is hard to know who is teaching whom sometimes, for Irene brings an unexpected sophistication and grasp of American culture's strengths and sillinesses, all at the same time, and often a keener eye to what works in human nature than anything Ottie's engineering education and man-of-the-world style can muster. He's a better shot, she's a better judge. They are a marvel together, and a constant joy to be with.

The idea for this book was a natural after Irene's many years of lecturing and writing, but I was unprepared for her insistence that we do *this* book together.

The honor has been mine, and the rewards endless, not least in knowing that I could at last bring a decade of study of the Upper Midwest Amish communities to bear on the story of Irene's life at Kalona, and do it real justice.

Yet for all my academic underpinnings in ethnic and religious studies, I remained in a constant relationship of education with Irene, fitting the truths of one woman's life inside an Amish community to a scholar's natural emotional detachment from her subject matter.

I had heard Irene lecture to a college Rural Sociology class and knew that we would bring a remarkably similar 'voice' to our expression, matching syntax and phrasing, semantics and a classic Upper Midwest inflection to our speech patterns that comes from our common geographic roots.

We wrote together in utter harmony, I setting up on the loom the framework of the book's substantive material as Irene spun out her personal narratives on the chapter subject. Warp and woof of a tapestry, I would finish her sentences, she would finish my paragraphs. I would write more narrative in her voice, she would supply substantive material in mine. Then we wove it all together so successfully that even Irene's husband Ottie was unable to tell, in the end, who's writing was whose.

It is not a perfect tapestry, not every expression of experience came easily. We celebrated our effort even while we struggled, for not all the chapters on Irene's life have happy endings, nor do they even now for the many women inside this most extraordinary of American cultural minorities.

But I believe we are greatly enriched when the simple veneer of a society is stripped away to reveal a truly rich—and remarkably complex—culture in which humans—just like ourselves—endeavor to make sense of the world in which they find themselves, and to be at peace with God.

If I take the wings of the morning, and dwell in the uttermost parts of the sea, even there shall Thy hand lead me.

I believe that these words of David's beautiful psalm can truly be said to be Irene's own watchwords of faith. She has moved out into the wider world of the English, surely in the company of Angels, wholeheartedly believing that her soul's salvation— once thought earnable only by works and deeds— could surely not be withheld from her. Indeed it has not, and she lives a life of active, loving, generous Christian faith every day in her home and in her church community.

Yet her departure from her Amish roots has cost her a great price: the *meidung*, the shunning, the utter loss of family and friends, and their confirmed belief that her soul is in peril, a price few of us are required in our lifetimes to pay, or could ever conceive of paying.

This book, then, seeks to educate both to the beauties and the challenges of life in the Amish world, as told by one who has lived this life, to one who has studied the cultures of the Plain People for many years.

For my part, I honor Irene.

For her part, the future holds great promise: life with Ottie, more books, certainly college, definitely children.

Also a continuing struggle with the concepts of space travel, prehistoric life, political campaigns, microwave ovens, and the Internet. Don't get me wrong: the girl runs rings around her husband when it comes to computers. Who do you think installs the new software packages on the home desktop system? Still, there are some concepts that come hard following a life of intense separation from the world.

But she deals, every day. Resilient and serene, Irene cherishes her life with Ottie and makes her way through the mazes and puzzles of English life one day at a time, managing to both make sense of—and sensible use of—our modern and oftimes bewildering ways, all the while celebrating our cherished national freedoms and our hard-earned civil liberties.

So stand back, be amazed, and celebrate with Irene.

I do. Every day. With joy.

Deborah Morse-Kahn

CHAPTER ONE

Kalona

Wherefore come out from among them, and be ye separate, saith the Lord...
I John 2:15

*I*was born Ruth Irene Miller on January 31st, 1974 to Alvin and Martha Miller in the Old Order Amish community at Kalona, Iowa. I was the second daughter and sixth of nine children, two of whom died in childhood. I had two names, the first after my grandmother Ruth and the second after my mom's friend Irene, but my parents were undecided which name they wanted to use. They called me "Girlie" until other people started calling me that and soon I became "Irene."

Kalona, settled in 1846, is one of twenty-eight Amish communities in Iowa and is the oldest existing Amish community west of the Mississippi. The first Amish to settle in Johnson/Washington County had to make their arduous journeys by oxcart and horse-cart across pioneer prairies in the years before the Civil War, younger sons leaving behind farms in Maryland and Pennsylvania in search of new land to raise crops and families.

My paternal grandparents, Tobias J. and Ruth Vanora Miller, settled in Kalona one hundred years later during the time of World War II. They had ten sons—Amos, Alvin, Elmer, Paul, Eldon, Simon, Jerry, Henry, Perry, and Earl— thus establishing what became a virtual dynasty of Miller families in the Kalona district as the sons grew to adulthood, married, and established farms and families of their own. In addition to my father Alvin's seven living children, I have *seventy-five* first cousins.

Amish families are by tradition and expectation quite large, and this number of first cousins is entirely normal. Because Amish families can be so large, and the same first and last names are so common, we rely very much on the middle name or initial to know which Miller is being spoken of. So it is very helpful that all of Grandpa Tobias' sons use the middle initial 'T.' The Miller sons became known as the 'T Boys' of Kalona!

My father and mother were married in 1963. Their first child, my brother Tobias ('Toby') A. Miller, was born a year later in 1964 but died in a childhood accident when he was three years old. My second brother, Elson, was born in 1966 and was very close to his older brother Toby and missed him terribly when he died. My older sister and the third child, Bertha, was born in 1967. Wilbur was born in 1969, Benedict ('Bendick') in 1971, then me in 1974, and Aaron in 1976. Baby Miriam lived only three hours in September 1980. The last child, Earl, was born in 1985.

Our Life at Kalona

The present day Town of Kalona and the surrounding Amish farmlands are set among the rolling green hills of Washington County eighteen miles to the south of Iowa City on State Highway 1. The town itself is small but the Amish settlements around the town expand the larger Kalona district to eight miles east, west and north of the town, with a combined population at just around 2,500, with some 200 Amish families represented. The Miller families together own hundreds of acres of this farmland.

Because our Amish settlement was one of the first in Iowa, it became as famous for drawing visitors as the nearby Amana Colonies did, and today draws thousands of tourists every year from all over the United States who drive among the many placid Amish family farms, visit the roadside workshops and stroll the town main street to browse in the many gift and antique shops that cater to visitors. The 'English' townfolk—to distinguish all non-Amish people—are entirely used to their Amish neighbors, and the tourism income is very welcome in this small farming community.

Kalona has regular craft, produce and horse auctions, and twice a year visitors pour in to attend the much larger quilt, furniture and craft auctions that feature Amish handwork. These auctions are very popular, and it is a time when English and some of Kalona's more liberal "Beachy" Amish and their Mennonite neighbors mix together freely through a long day of auction activity and browsing the open warehouse floor filled with beautiful quilt displays, handsome handcrafted home and yard furniture, children's toys, hanging baskets overflowing with greenhouse flowers and vines, and tables piled with baked goods.

The Amish will set up snack and lunch services at their Amish farm auctions and cook up some of our traditional foods for the English and Amish visitors alike, serving from early morning through late afternoon, until the last of the food has been dished up. At the end of the day they have raised enough money to take care of those in need in their community, those who have been ill or hospitalized or have lost homes or livestock during the year. They will also have baked goods available to visitors.

Farming for the Amish is a lifetime occupation, and the work they believe God wants for them. The Amish use the same traditional agricultural methods used for hundreds of years, employing crop rotation, manure for fertilizer, limited use of chemical applications, and drawing machinery and equipment by horsepower.

The Kalona Amish community also has several small stores on the farms that are run by families that also raise crops or dairy cattle. These stores sell such things as bulk foods which we like to use in our special recipes, as well as the fabrics in colors that we want for our clothing. We take our horses to the blacksmith down the road, have our buggies repaired, harness rewoven, and small gasoline engines repaired by our Amish neighbors. We like to patronize our community's businesses as much as possible.

Of course, Kalona's main street has many services that the Amish routinely use for everyday needs. We have individual family bank accounts like most English do, and shop for hardware and groceries in town every week if not more often. The town of Kalona has several hitching post sites for its Amish citizens: a large one with good shelter for many buggies on the south part of town behind the bank, and a smaller open-rail spot on the east part of town next to the hardware store, with room for eight buggies.

If we need a doctor or dentist, chiropractor or optician, or need to go to one of the larger retail stores like Wal-Mart for bulk supplies, we will arrange in advance for an 'Amish taxi' ride by car or van into the larger communities like Iowa City or Washington. The Amish will ride in automobiles at need but not own them: they believe the material burden would be too great, and automobiles would only encourage easier and faster travel, and at a greater distance from home.

The streets of Kalona are well paved and maintained but, as you move out of town and into the farmlands, the horse-and-buggies are soon trotting on gravel roads. My family's farm is located just about a mile outside of town and is entirely surrounded by other Amish farms.

Traditional Amish farms average around 100 acres, considered a perfect farm size that can be managed by one family. A farm this size can produce enough food for a year, to be eaten fresh or canned and put up for the winter months.

All of my Kalona uncles farmed as the main source of income. My grandfather had a sawmill and he also had a business where he sold tin to use for roofing and siding. My uncle Earl who lived on the same farm did the farming and helped with the business. My uncle Eldon dappled in other businesses besides farming. He had chicken houses, bought real estate and sold it for subdivisions, and did a few other things such as raising pumpkins for the Hy-Vee food stores in Iowa.

According to our church rules, the *Ordnung* (ohrd'-noong), our community of Amish families was not supposed to participate in The Kalona Fall Festival, Kalona Days, Quilt Shows, etc., but having non-farming activities such as buggy shops, furniture shops, and grocery and variety stores was acceptable. Also, the Amish in our community didn't try to attract tourists like some Amish communities, so we didn't have the huge flea markets or produce and quilt auctions like some do.

We often had English visitors, sometimes more distant neighbors stopping by, sometimes folks wanting to buy eggs or other produce. Of course, the feedman and milk tanker truck driver came by regularly, as did English people who brought their horses to be shod or trained by my brother.

At different times over the years English friends of our family would come to the farm for the day and help in the fields simply because it was how their fathers and their grandfathers farmed. The Amish routinely help any neighbor in need as well. Also we would see fruit peddlers stop by in the summer months offering us additional fruit to buy—watermelons, cantaloupe, peaches and apples. Like most Amish families we had a large fruit orchard, but if the growing season was poor we sometimes would not have enough of our own produce to put up for family use in the coming winter months.

As with many Amish communities around the United States, we had Mennonite neighbors. The Mennonites, with their acceptance of modern conveniences, often have provided a middle ground between the Old Order Amish and their English neighbors. The Mennonites sprang from the same Anabaptist ('adult baptism') religious traditions but, as with the Amish, took a more modern path in their chosen lifestyles.

We had Mennonite neighbors and used their telephone when we had need. They would deliver important phone messages about a birth or a death from other communities and in turn we were glad to do favors for them such as sharing baked goods or fresh orchard fruits in the summertime. If there was a birth in their family, we would dress and walk over for a Sunday afternoon visit, just as we would with our fellow Amish neighbors. We would hire Mennonites as well as English drivers to take us to distant weddings, funerals or to visit family out-of-state.

Our Amish community in Kalona was of the kind of Amish called "Old Order." This distinguishes us from other Amish groups that want a more conservative—or a more liberal—way of life while still holding to the basic religious precepts of the Amish Faith.

Sometimes the differences cannot be easily determined by the English: the size of a hat brim, hooks-and-eyes to fasten clothing, the color of a buggy. Many times the differences are confusing even to us: the most conservative of the Amish, the Swartzentruber (swahrtzen'-troober) Amish who live mostly in southwestern Wisconsin and southeastern Minnesota, are by far much more conservative in their clothing and buggies but often far more liberal in allowing their youth to roam from Amish ways in late adolescence, the time of *rumspringe*, the "running around time."

All the Amish groups have critical beliefs in common: that farming is the chosen way of life, followed by carpentry, Jesus' family's work; that horse culture is the mainstay of an agricultural life; that modern conveniences are to be avoided lest they distract us from the plain life; that men and women have distinctly different roles and tasks, both in the family and in the community; and that the *Ordnung*, the rules of our church, are the foundation of the community.

What changes a great deal from community to community is the nature and content of the *Ordnung*. One Amish community may hold a somewhat different *Ordnung* –more conservative, or more liberal—than an Amish community in another town, or another state. Indeed, it is common for an Amish family to move to a new community to take advantage of that difference in church rules, depending on what they believe is right.

What is common to all Amish communities, however, is the *meidung* (my'-duhng), a form of social avoidance that the English know as shunning. The Amish would say a person is "in the ban." Shunning is seen by the Amish as a severe and final form of correction applied to someone who has moved away from the *Ordnung*, from the rules of the church as that community defines them. When someone from our community was shunned, it was total and community-wide; indeed as word would be communicated to family members far away, Amish communities in other states would impose the *meidung* on the shunned person.

The *meidung* is a terribly difficult concept for most English to understand, much less accept. There are Amish, also, who grow to find they too cannot agree with this most severe of Amish church precepts.

However, if they leave to live among the English, shunning is immediately imposed and fiercely maintained in the hope that the wayward soul will repent and return to live peaceably among the Amish once again.

Chapter Two

"A New Little Dishwasher"

But every woman that prayeth or prophesieth with
her head uncovered dishonoreth her head.
- 1 Cor 11:5

I began my life in a tradition of faith and culture that believed that works and deeds brought salvation, that the roles of men and women were prescribed by God, that intentional separation from the outside world was the mainstay of our philosophy, and that a plain life—shunning adornments and all matters of the material world that was not utterly necessary for a plain life—was holy before God.

To bend in humility before God, to work toward the common needs and the common goals, and to raise one's children to understand their responsibilities in a culture where works and deeds were paramount was the highest good.

Above all else, Amish life is about family life. The hundreds of letters from correspondents writing to the weekly Amish national newspapers *The Budget* and *Die Botschaft* (dee boat'-shahft) ('The Message') list all births in their home communities as well as news about visitors, those who have wed, those who are ill, and those who have died.

The Amish cherish and welcome children into family life, and we can immediately understand the distinctive ways in which baby girls ("new little dishwashers") and boys ("new little woodchoppers") are mentioned by the writers, showing how children are raised in clear role models for their lives as members of large families who make their living from the land, and who will die in good faith with a church that asks each of us to fulfill our duties on earth with simplicity and humility.

Though Amish children are individuals in their own right, with their own real choices and needs, so also are Amish children needed to fulfill their roles in the family. We learn at a very early age the tasks we are destined for, and the skills we need to do those tasks.

It is for the eldest children that the first real burdens come, as they quickly learn that they must help their mother and father—and later their many younger siblings—by taking up what tasks they can, and accepting those tasks as fit for their gender and their responsibilities in their community.

There is great emphasis placed on appropriate roles for girls and for boys. From the earliest age, gentle training and role-playing by parents and older siblings ushers the children into the present and future that their age and their gender dictate in Amish life.

In a life of farming— whether field crops or vegetable gardens, dairy cattle or horses, goats, sheep, chickens, or pigs—the boys and girls learn to sort out their tasks and come to an early understanding that it is both their privilege and duty that they do their very best.

In Amish life, the girls are found working at tasks in and

around the home. We learn to help in preparing meals at a very young age, and are taught how to keep the household neat and clean. We watch to learn how vegetables, fruits and meats are canned and stored for the long winter months. We sweep and mop, wash and dry dishes, bake breads and start the next meal in the oven. We spend a long day over laundry, washing an entire family's clothing with our homemade lye-based laundry soap. We then pass it through the Maytag wringer which is powered by a gasoline engine (the Swartzentruber Amish use a hand-cranked wringer), and then peg it out to dry in any season, to be folded and put away later.

At sunrise the girls as well as the boys have risen and dressed, and made their way out to the barns to help with milking the cows and feeding the horses and pigs. The boys will stay in the barns to continue their work there while the girls make their way back to the kitchen to help with breakfast table setting and meal serving. Most families will then kneel in family prayer as the father prays from the *Christenpflicht*, the Amish prayerbook. They then take their morning meal—bowing heads in a silent prayer of thanks—then wash and clean, and go on to their morning tasks or, for the older children, walk or be taken by buggy to school. Though our family always took breakfast together, in some Amish families fathers and sons may eat before daughters and mothers, leaving shortly afterwards for the fieldwork and the barns.

For seven months of the year, girls and their mothers work in the vegetable garden and the orchard, tending the many fresh vegetables and fruits that are a large part of our self-sustaining life. Preparing soil, planting seeds and seedlings, hoeing and raking, weeding and watering, mulching, pruning and picking continue on through the late spring, summer and autumn months. Seasonal crops are harvested and canned or bottled for stores, and the old roots are grubbed out to make room for the next round of planting in the garden.

Many families have greenhouses in addition to gardens and orchards, and this too is women's work, carefully potting and fostering flowering baskets and garden annuals to sell at the local produce auctions. Extra vegetable plants such as tomato and zucchini are also set aside for these popular weekly sales. Some greenhouses are large enough to be established as independent businesses, and these are traditionally run by the women in the family.

Preparations for a noon meal are begun by midmorning. For our family, my father and brothers brought the horses in from the fields to be watered and fed, and we would sit down together for the noon dinner. In some Amish families, if fathers and brothers are in the fields, the dinner pails and lemonade are brought out to wherever they are and the meal taken sitting by the patient horses and idled field machinery. Sometimes sisters and mothers will eat with them but more often they return to the house to wash up, consider the evening meal, and begin the afternoon's work.

If this was a time for butchering—pigs or chickens—then this all-day work would begin in earnest with many hands helping, and the Amish learn early as children that farm animals are a source of food for us. Canning the meat quickly follows the butchering and new rows of gleaming jars soon appear in the basement storeroom.

If there are no large tasks to be done, the afternoon is a time for sewing or mending, various household repairs, or hitching up one of the trotters to take the buggy into town for shopping. Sometimes visitors stop by from neighboring farms, or there would be errands run to neighbors to exchange fresh produce or baked goods, look in on someone who was ill, or just exchange news of friends and family.

The evening meal is much like the morning meal: the entire family will sit down together to offer a prayer of thanks, eat supper, and talk about the day. After supper the girls again wash up and the boys return to the barns once more to settle the farm animals in for the night. Studying, reading and playing with toys by kerosene lamplight in the winter months, or by late-setting sun in the summer months, pass the evening hours until bedtime. Popcorn is a usual snack before bedtime, especially in the wintertime.

Life in Our Family

At home on our farm we were trained in the tasks that were expected of us, both as family members, and as boys or girls. As a family we all helped each other with whatever had to be done. For example, hay had to be put up between rains, oats had to be harvested when it was ripe, and the silo had to be filled when the corn was at a certain stage, so everyone pitched in to help.

Making hay was done by the family, but thrashing oats and filling silos was a neighborhood event. The families in our neighborhood shared the thrashing machine and as it moved from farm to farm the menfolk in that 'thrasher ring' would all help each other until the thrashing was done. When the men came to our farm to help thrash our oats, my mom, sister, and I spent all day cooking mountains of food and washing dishes. We would also have to keep the water jugs filled with water and my youngest brother was the 'waterboy,' carrying the waterjugs out by pony to the working men in the fields. Before the men left for home they were served a refreshing snack, such as watermelon or pie.

When the fruit in the orchard ripened, the fruit had to be canned before it spoiled. During those times, Dad and a couple of my brothers would help us if their own work could wait. Or if the fruit peddler came by with peaches, they would help peel them and fill the jars. During canning season or butchering, when the women were extra busy, my dad would sometimes wash the dishes after supper.

We children were taught to interact with each other as peacefully as possible but, naturally, we had our share of squabbles. If we quarreled over playing with a certain toy by proclaiming "we had it first" the toy might be taken away altogether until we could share nicely. Other forms of discipline when we misbehaved were sitting on a chair or standing with our nose in the corner until our parents told us we could go.

The Amish fully believe in corporal punishment and there was a two-foot leather strap on a shelf in the coat closet that was brought out and used depending on the offense, a very severe form of punishment indeed. My father used it more often than I believe many parents did and so I have many unhappy memories of being disciplined, or knowing my siblings were being disciplined, in such a way.

My mother was pretty shrewd—and much gentler—when it came to discipline. She told me how one of my brothers, when he was quite small, had such an awful habit of biting his siblings and other children when they upset him. She said she tried spanking and everything else she could think of but nothing worked. One day he bit a child so hard it drew blood! My mom decided to give him (literally!) a taste of his own medicine and she said later that he looked so shocked, having figured out that biting *hurt*, and he never did it again.

Now as for me, I gave her fits as well. She told me how I had such a bad temper and when I was upset I didn't get over it easily. She said she tried spanking and other methods but none of them worked except for one thing and I still remember having to do this: I had to sit in a chair and I could not get out to play again until I could *sing*. As you can imagine, singing was the *last* thing I felt like doing! I remember vividly how frustrating that was. You cannot sing and be angry at the same time! Here was a much gentler and loving form of discipline.

My brothers hated doing 'girls work,' but because there were more boys than girls in the family, and the younger boys didn't have the responsibilities that my older brothers had, they had to help with the dishes after meals and also with some tasks during canning season. The noon meal was always a very big production and generated so many dirty dishes that I hated to do dishes as much as they did! We would edge our way to the door as casually as possible and then make a wild dash for the dirt lane that led to the field at the back of our property so to be well out of earshot before we could be called back!

My brothers and I would mow the yard, and help hoe and cultivate the garden in the summertime along with other duties we could do. However, for an Amish family that has more girls than boys, girls would fill the farming roles in field and barn and work just like boys.

Of course...we played! My brothers and I played in the haymow: we climbed into the half-empty silo to yell and hear the echo, or we climbed up into the holding bins to play in the corn or oats. We also played 'horse-and-buggy' by riding in the garden cart like a 'buggy' and the one pulling was the 'horse.'

My brother Elson would rig up a swing in the barn's vast empty haymow (the place where all the hay bales or loose hay was stored for the cattle) using the rope and pulleys that would later be used to haul the hay up. Then we would climb up to the top of the 14-foot bin next to the haymow, get set into the swing, and jump off into empty space. It was wild!

After watching Elson break horses, we imitated the unruly horses and the 'driver' had to correct his 'horse.' We imitated him by shoeing each other as well. Mom used scrap denim and made a double harness for us and it worked out great. Two of us were the 'team of horses' and the other the 'driver.' We even made fun out of work in the summertime by the 'team' pulling the cultivator and the 'driver' pushing and guiding it between the rows.

Elson was somewhat of a prankster. One evening at dusk when it was footwashing time before going to bed, Elson covered up with a white sheet and came running around the corner of the house and scared the living daylights out of us. He would scare my sister after dark when she was washing dishes by unexpectedly jumping in front of the window, making faces and yelling.

The best was the day Elson, Bertha, and I were going to our widowed Amish neighbor to take her a cake and food and sing for her. (In the summertime, Benedict, Aaron, and I would quite often take her food and sing her a few songs.) She lived in the little house of her "English" son's farm and he had electric fences. Elson grabbed the fence briefly and looked at Bertha and said, "It didn't shock me so it must not be hot." Bertha was skeptical so he grabbed it again.

Convinced, Bertha took hold of the fence, screamed, jumped off the ground, and dropped the cake. The cake was a bit shaken, but all right because it was wrapped up. Elson had a good laugh and then explained how he listened for the pulses running through the fence and that he touched it between the pulses. My other brothers were ornery in different but similar ways, teasing their sisters with snakes, frogs, and creepy insects.

We younger children went barefoot in the barn when we milked the cows. We would run down the dirt lane that led to the pasture to bring the cows in for milking. We had to bring them home at a leisurely walk because calm cows give more milk. This gave us plenty of time to goof off. We would sometimes step into the fresh cow pies to feel it squish between our toes (some said it helped heal any little cuts or wounds on one's foot). We would usually wash it off when we got back to the barn or else it would dry and would be hard to get off.

Our dog Patsy, a Blue Heeler with a deep black coat, would understand the Pennsylvania Dutch, or *Deutsche* (doytch) phrase *Gal Hola*! "Get the horses!" While my brother Elson rode to the back fields where the horses were, Patsy got there long before and waited for him at the gate. Then all Elson had to do was give her the command and she would round the horses up and, nipping at their heels, would bring them back to the barn at full gallop, enjoying every moment!

Plain People, Plain Dress

Though there are many more 'plain peoples' besides the Amish in the Upper Midwest—Mennonites, Wilburite Quakers, River Brethren, Hutterite, and Old Order German Baptist Brethren also have settled in Iowa, Minnesota and Wisconsin—it is by the appearance of their clothing that the English most quickly recognize the Amish: solid colors, hats and caps, bonnets and shawls, aprons and fall-front pants, suspenders and dark hose and dark shoes.

Though it would not be easily discerned by the English observer, within the national Amish community are many subgroups of Amish who dress somewhat differently from each other to underscore a more conservative, or more liberal, *Ordnung*, or church rule.

Thus, from the most conservative Swartzentruber Amish to the most liberal New Order or Beachy Amish, you will find great variation on hat brims, hooks-and-eyes vs. straight pins vs. buttons, one suspender (crossed over the shoulder) vs. two, higher hems or lower, puffed sleeves (Pennsylvania) or plain

(Iowa), black laced shoes or Nike running shoes, full white ba-
tiste prayer *kapps* (prayer caps) with tie strings or smaller ones
with looped strings.

What changes least is color use: for the men as well as for
the women, shirts and dresses can display rich blue, deep green,
purple, maroon, or gray. Men's pants are universally black, or
dark denim blue. Women's shawls and men's coats are also
black. Men will sometimes wear shorter jackets of dark denim
blue. Straw hats serve for men in the summertime, and women
will wear solid color kerchiefs. The Amish women make most
of their family clothing, but shoemaking is not an Amish art so
families will go into town to buy shoes. Also, men's black felt
hats are ordered from Amish haberdashers; women will sew
their own bonnets and prayer *kapps*.

Acceptable clothing for young girls usually imitates those
of the older women, though there is more flexibility allowed
in colors.

As a child I wore medium to dark colored dresses that buttoned in the back. On Sundays and when we went to town, I
wore a pinafore-type garment over the dress, one that almost
encircled my whole body. It had openings in the front for my
arms to go through and it buttoned in the back as well. Along
with that, I wore black shoes and stockings and a white or black
kapp over my braided hair.

We were allowed to go barefoot in the spring when we saw
a bumblebee, an indication that not only did it feel warm
enough, the ground was actually warm enough. We went barefoot everywhere we could and donned an old pair of shoes only
when we had to go through a field that had thistles or stubble

that made it hard to walk. We got new shoes once a year in the autumn when the weather turned cool and they lasted until spring when we could go barefoot again. As children we went to church and school barefoot, but if we went to town or a public place we wore shoes.

I remember having a pink 'everyday' dress that was a hand-me-down and I believe was a dress my mother had worn. I liked my pink dress and I remember my siblings teasing me by saying "pink-stink"!

I probably started wearing a head covering all the time around the age of four; little girls including babies always wear one in church. The head coverings looked like my Mother's and the other adult women, just a smaller version made to fit.

Though all Amish clothing is plain—without adornment—the most important article of clothing is the hat for men and the cap, or _kapp_, for women. It fulfills God's commandment that we have our heads covered in God's presence as a sign of humility. Thus, even the youngest boy will not go out into the larger community without his black felt or straw hat, and no girl will go without a headcovering at any time, usually her white muslin crimped prayer _kapp_; even for field work she will wear a kerchief, and some very conservative Amish church districts require that women wear a _kapp_ even for sleep.

Many religious communities, including Orthodox Jews and Muslims, have such a proscription against an uncovered head. The Amish learn early to accept and expect a head covering at all times (though, interestingly, only the women are required to keep the _kapp_ on during worship: men do remove their hats.)

Only the style of hat or *kapp*—broad brim or small, high crown or low, bonnet strings or none at all—will mark the difference among the Amish to their neighbors.

CHAPTER THREE

Growing Up Amish

Therefore the Lord God sent him forth from the Garden of
Eden to till the soil from whence he was taken.
- Gen 3:23

Life on any farm in America is bound to the seasons of the year and, in this 21st century of American agriculture, the Amish farm fully reflects today what all farm life was surely like one hundred years ago.

Every season, and every month of the season, has its special accorded rituals and tasks. No matter that the Amish farmer grows major crops for sale, or raises dairy cattle for milk, or has built a carpentry industry and grows produce for the regional auctions; all must bend to the season's shift and change, in times of good weather and bad, good crop prices or poor, good health or ill. The Amish family is bound together for the seasonal journey and the members of Amish families—indeed the entire community— look to one another for support and comfort.

The child growing up on an Amish farm is almost always one of a great many siblings; it has always been this way in Amish life and remains so today, most notable in a time when most American families no longer raise large families.

Interdependency in an Amish family is wanted, cultivated and supported, so that none may feel they are without the work God would wish them to have, and that none may feel alone. In a culture which teaches that the soul's salvation comes not through Grace but through honorable work and deeds pursued with a full heart, one's work becomes one's life, and the Amish lesson is that the detail of that work is of far less importance than work done cheerfully and with humility.

Children's work in Amish daily life is not only greatly valued, it is greatly needed. The youngest children are given toys and playthings which model the life to come: toy farm animals and wagons, dollies to care for and miniature cookware to fashion make-believe bread and pies. Children's books tell stories about farm life, about helping their mother and father, about being good to one's siblings, about school days, and about the martyrs of the Anabaptist faith hundreds of years ago in Europe, before the Amish sought religious freedom in America. Children are given ponies, lambs, chicks and calves to care for in preparation for later responsibilities. By the time even the youngest child is being taught to spread grain for the chickens or feed the goats, they have already learned a great deal about their place in the Amish family.

As Amish children grow older the skills they are taught become increasingly sophisticated, and greater responsibility is placed upon them. Between the ages of eight and fifteen, Amish children are balancing home life, school life and church life expectations.

Farm and household work responsibilities grow and children become responsible for specific jobs (much as an English child would to earn their allowance). School-age children are expected to take their reading, writing and arithmetic seriously for the years in which they are required to take class: at age fourteen, at the end of eighth grade, by American law they are permitted to leave school and take up their life on the family farm in earnest, or to "work away" to earn money for the family.

Young people who work off the family farm turn all their money back to their father until the child reaches the age of twenty-one: then, they are permitted to keep their own money. When a young man reaches the age of twenty-one, or marries, his father will usually purchase him a new buggy, a horse and a harness set; a young woman would receive a piece of home furnishing such as a hutch, or a chest. In our family the tradition was that our father would also open a bank account in our names when we turned twenty-one, and put $500 in it.

Twice-monthly church Sundays are a very sober worship experience and even the youngest child is taught what is expected of them and helped to know their role and place in the community worship experience.

Through all these experiences of home, school and worship runs the constant theme of *interdependence*: among family members, among neighbors, among community, always to be remembered and accorded with good will and humility, never to be set aside. Such interdependence—a community quality which most clearly calls to the wistful English observer— is the very fabric of Amish life and, in its culture of works and deeds, the highest calling for hope of salvation in the Amish church.

That aid is always available, no matter the cause, brings a quality of comfort and assurance to Amish life that would be hard to replicate in the outside English world. But it is also very important to note that, where a culture relies on the interdependence of each and every individual, where a culture teaches that one's salvation is intertwined with one's neighbors, there can be over-strict vigilance for the souls of others. Many disagreements in Amish life arise over the issues of humble compliance with the *Ordnung*—the church rules— and it is the unwillingness to live among others who are—in some minds—far too interested in the good comportment of others that causes families to pull up roots and find a more forgiving—read *liberal*—settlement in which to live. Reports to the ministers or even to the bishop of the supposed misconduct of a neighbor can become insupportable: to avoid confrontation—which is anathema in Amish life—those wishing a more forgiving approach to salvation through works and deeds will quietly find themselves a new home elsewhere.

The Year on the Miller Farm

Our family life flowed in a great sweep from early spring to late winter, year passing year. Because my father was entirely devoted to the farming life and did not pursue craft or milling work, all of our family tasks were given over to growing—horses, cattle, chickens, pigs, large crops, small crops—and using what we grew.

We had two large vegetable gardens and a strawberry patch, with extra growing space for corn and potatoes. Next to these were grape arbors and fruit orchards where we grew several types of apples, apricots, pears, cherries, plums, and peaches. When we would get home from school we would stop at the grape arbor just behind the evergreen trees near the road and help ourselves to an after-school "snack!"

As we younger children began to grow up we left the strict confines of the expected tasks of boys and girls and were needed to become useful in a much larger range of farming skills.

On our own family's farm I primarily helped my mother with household and yard work, but I always helped with the milking, and when I got older, I also helped with some field work. I helped husk corn by hand and at times drove the tractor that pulled the baler while one of my brothers stacked the bales on the wagon.

I would also take our team of Percheron draft horses hooked to a two-wheeled cart and pull wagonloads of hay from the field to the barn. We didn't use an elevator to get the hay to the haymow so loads of hay were pulled into the haymow by fork and rope on pulleys. My dad or brother would stick the hay fork and I would drive the team to pull the hay into the mow. Someone was in the mow to stack the bales and at times when help was short, I would help stack the bales after the wagon was unloaded.

I started milking a cow at six or seven years old and we would practice on the ones that were easy to milk or almost dry and didn't give a lot of milk. As we got better we would sit on the opposite side of the cow someone else was milking. When the older person got done with his side, he would finish our side. Along with helping to milk a cow or two, we had chores such as gathering the eggs and feeding the bottle to the little calves.

On a typical summer day Dad would call our names from the bottom of the stairs to wake us at 5:15 A.M. When we got to the barn the cows were waiting to be milked and usually went to their proper stalls but we'd have to guide the ones that didn't. The ground feed that was put before them in the trough helped them behave. We put a chain around their necks once they were in their stall to keep them there, gave them some hay as well, and we'd tie up their tails away from our faces so they couldn't swat us while we milked them. A scraper was used to move the manure that they had dragged in into the gutters.

There were two rows of stalls with a broad center part in the middle where we rolled the heavy-duty cart loaded with milk buckets, hobbles and one-legged milk stools. The big engine was started up on the compressor that cooled the milk in the bulk tank that sat in the milkhouse. One of the lids on the tank was removed and a strainer was placed in the opening.

We would get the cow ready to be milked by washing her teats and udder after putting a pair of hobbles on her hind legs to prevent her from moving around. Two people helped each other, one on each side of her to milk the cows that gave a lot of milk. We got more milk if we got the milk out fast, and the best dairy cows filled five-gallon buckets when they were "fresh," when they had just had calves and were in peak production.

As we filled our buckets with milk, we carried them to the milk-house and emptied them into the strainer to filter out any dirt. If there were calves, we fed them a bottle while the rest finished milking.

We were around the big draft horses at a young age when we were on the wagon with our brothers or dad, but we knew to keep our distance from their hind ends. My brothers hitched them up as soon as they were tall enough or strong enough to do so but drove them sooner than that. At the age of six Elson drove the team of 2,000-pound Percheron draft horses hitched to a wagon of corn into Kalona to get the corn ground at the feed mill. It is not uncommon for the Amish to put their very young children in charge of the largest farm animals.

Butchering was a family event and we had jobs we could do according to our age. As children we would watch the slaughter of an animal: if it was a pig or cow, we were too small to help dress the carcass and prepare it for butchering, but when the meat was being processed we could help cut some meat off the bones, carry jars, etc. As for the chickens, we could help pluck their feathers, wash them and pick all the fine stubble off while mom and my sister gutted them and cut them up. I would watch this process and I started doing the same at probably nine or ten years old.

In the wintertime, when my siblings and I got home from school, our chores were to gather the eggs, haul firewood from the wood-house, carry it to the wood-box for the stove that heated the house, and fill the lamps and lanterns with fuel. We had the gas lanterns to use in the barn for chores and for the main part of the house. Kerosene lamps with their softer light were used in the bedrooms and bathroom.

Suppers in the wintertime consisted of hot soup such as

chicken noodle soup, chili, or 'rivel' (noodle dumpling) soup along with homemade bologna sandwiches, egg sandwiches, or hot dogs, which was a treat. Sometimes we topped off the meal with cherry cobbler, apple crisp, and occasionally homemade ice cream. A bigger treat was store-bought ice cream!

Sometimes instead of having soup, Mom cooked a huge pot of hot corn mush that we ate with milk and the leftovers were a real treat. The remaining mush was put in a baking dish and for breakfast it was sliced and fried and served with honey or molasses and oh, was that good!

Playtime on the Farm

Playtime in the winter before bedtime was so much fun! We lived on the best sledding hill and we had a pond so all the neighbor children came to our farm to go sledding or ice skating. When the weather wasn't right for sledding or skating, Dad would sometimes join us in our play, teaching us some of his boyhood games.

Our family really had no pets besides the farm animals, and you learned at an early age not to get attached to them as pets because they were expendable. They were either on the food chain or destroyed if they were of no value or became a nuisance.

We had a female farm dog that had puppies nearly every year and we loved playing with them when they were old enough although we knew all of them had to go. Having more than one farm dog is not a good thing if you want high quality so all our dog's puppies had to be given away to those in the community who wanted a farm dog. The puppies that weren't adopted were gently put down. Puppies that grow to adulthood and don't turn out to be good farm dogs face the same fate.

Kittens were born to our barn cats every year and we played with them as well. Cats were animals that existed on the farm not so much for a particular purpose but they found their own food and I'm sure they kept the mice population down around the outbuildings.

I was a tomboy, spending most of my playtime with my brothers. Instead of playing with dolls, I would much rather play with the kittens and puppies. I spent a lot of time playing with them as my 'babies' and would sing and rock them to sleep. Sometimes we played 'church' with them: one of my brothers did the 'preaching' and my other brother and me were the 'parents,' the puppies or kittens being our 'children.'

My brother Earl was born when I was eleven and I was overjoyed to have a real baby in the family! I was a baby-lover and all my friends seem to have babies in the family except us and I was envious. Someone in town teased Dad about him and Mom being Abraham and Sarah because of their age. I loved caring and playing with Earl but I also had to wash his dirty diapers! As he got older, we were pretty close as well. If I was in deep thought, he would grin and say "Peenie is sad." (When we were little, "Peenie" was a name Benedict called me when he was upset with me.)

We never had birthday parties because parties weren't allowed. For fun, the traditional thing to do for a birthday was to spank the person as many times as their age and stuff them under the table! Of course the birthday person had fun trying to keep it from happening, but impossible if the family ganged up on you. Thankfully, as you got older this wasn't done as much!

My mom had a decorating kit from a baking company and it was used to make the birthday cakes as fancy as possible. We could always expect ice cream and a homemade cake that Mom decorated especially for us. She'd try to keep the cake hidden from the birthday person until it was time to eat it.

My birthday came just one day before my brother Elson's, so sometimes the cake was decorated with both our names on it and our birthdays were celebrated together. We had ice cream twice and there was enough cake left from the day before.

One highlight for my siblings and me was getting a card from our Indiana grandparents with $5 inside. We really didn't expect a gift from our parents, but Mom usually tried to have a little something special made for our birthdays, such as a pair of gloves, coat, or a piece of clothing we needed. The item may not even be given on our birthday and it was never a wrapped gift that was opened before the whole family.

I don't ever remember giving my parents a gift for their birthday but as my sister and I got old enough we would bake and decorate a cake for them to go with the ice cream.

As each of my siblings reached their significant independence milestone of age twenty-one, we invited the cousins to our house for supper and games. Of course we had the usual, birthday cake and ice cream, and if it was summertime we may have played volleyball.

When I turned twenty-one, Elson and his wife Loretta

hosted my "cousin birthday supper." I had worked for them quite a bit as they had their children and we had grown very close. Several of my cousins didn't come because there was complaining among some in the community about *any* birthday celebrations because they were too much like a *party*.

Girls are luckier than boys when it comes to birthdays it seems. In school my girlfriends and I exchanged cards and small gifts like pretty handkerchiefs, homemade yarn pot-holders, key chains, and such.

As an older teen, when I joined the *junge* (yoong'-ee)—literally 'the young folks'— it was the same, but my circle of friends was now larger and I would get quite a few gifts, usually pieces of pretty glassware like candy dishes, salt and pepper-shakers, toothpick holders, or pretty decorative serving dishes. All the gifts were appropriate for future housekeeping and my sister and I displayed our dishes in a china cabinet in our room.

I got quite a few cards through the mail from pen pals or from girls in my circle letter. Writing letters is the main source of personal contact between friends and family, and circle letters are ways for groups of people—families, or cousins, or friends who share the same birth year—to keep in touch. One person starts the letter and sends it on to the next person on the list, who adds their own news, and sends it on again. The circle is complete when the first person on the list receives news from the last person on the list. Their old letter is then taken out and a new one takes its place for the next round.

My dad had several circle letters and mom had a sibling circle letter (she had ten brothers and sisters who lived in Indiana). My dad wrote letters to friends quite often, including his letters as "scribe" to one of our two national Amish-Mennonite newspapers, *Die Botschaft* (the other newspaper is *The Budget*). He probably wrote several hand-written letters a week, especially in the wintertime when things weren't so busy.

I had several circle letters and early on I wrote letters to friends out-of-state, the daughters of those families who had come to visit at our house.

I believe it was for my twenty-first birthday I got fifty-one birthday cards from my friends!

Work as Play

When I was old enough to be really helpful to my mother I was allowed to be part of the quilting *frolics* (gatherings) where the girls and women of a community would come together to spend the afternoon working communally on quilt work, often to raise money for a family that had experienced hard times, or to help pay the medical expenses for someone who was ill or injured. Quilts always brought a good price in Kalona. The city has held an annual Quilt Show for a quarter of a century, drawing thousands of visitors to the town. Kalona is known as the Quilt Capital of Iowa.

Though it is very common for the adult women in an Amish community to have quiltings, as I got older going to the gatherings together became less frequent. My mother was a very kind and loving person and was the "doctor" in the family, and she had a lot of people in the community—both Amish and English—come to see her on a regular basis for foot reflexology and healing massages. So over the years my mother was in-

Notice the fringed shawl the woman is wearing while she is in town shopping. The shawl is a required garment worn by young and adult women. Holmes County, Ohio.

A young married couple in Cave City, KY.

Swartzentruber Amish boys near Kidron, Ohio. Amish children begin driving the family's trusted horse at an early age.

A long walk home from school

Returning home from a long trip

Swartzentruber Amish women at an Amish farm auction in Munfordville, KY.

Shopping trip to town with the children.

Young Amish woman at work in the corn field near Montgomery, Indiana.

Ethridge, Tennessee

On a shopping trip in Glasgow, KY.

Roadside picnic lunch for Kalona Iowa Amish.

Children near Georgetown, Pennsylvania on roller blades, another mode of transportation allowed in some communities.

Children in Ohio going home from school.

Young Swartzentruber Amish women attending an Amish farm sale in Claire, Michigan.

Old Order Amish women at an auction in Claire, Michigan

Young people dressed in work clothes near Mt. Hope, Ohio.

Amish of Munfordville, KY at a sale.

Mesmerized by the camera, Apple Creek, Ohio.

Swartzentruber Amish children playing with a hand-crafted wagon. Notice the style of the little boy's hair cut, used only in certain communities.

The beginning of a new school year for these children in Glasgow, KY.

creasingly busy giving healing treatments to clients, and I was increasingly busy taking care of the housework because by then my sister Bertha was twenty-one and on her own away from the family.

Alas, my sister and I didn't always get along very well. She was six years older than I was and I think that was the biggest problem. I was a fiery independent sort that didn't want to take orders from my "bossy older sister" and the more she insisted, the more I rebelled! This caused a lot of squabbles between us, of course. As in most Amish families, my sister and I shared the same room and bed at night and my brothers shared a room and beds, so we couldn't even escape at bedtime!

Quilting and frolics are only just some of the kinds of work-as-play gatherings that the Amish organize: the barn-raisings for which the English admire the Amish so greatly are known as *barn frolics* and many families around the community will also have frolics to bring many hands together to lay building foundations, put up large outbuildings, repair storm damage, or bring in crops for a family seeing hard times.

While in many Amish communities items such as quilts are made to be sold to the English shops in town, in our community at Kalona our sewings produced quilts and comforters for charity, in particular for the needy in Eastern European countries.

The Amish and Mennonites in America have long supported international crisis needs giving time, skills and money through activities such as the Mennonite Relief, Mennonite Disaster Service and Christian Aid Ministries fairs, where a full day of events open to the English community raises goods and donations to be sent overseas. In Kalona, the Christian Aid Ministries have opened a depot for clothing donations, and the Amish and Mennonite families in the community come to help sort and bale the donated items and get them ready to be shipped out to places such as Haiti, Costa Rica, Romania and other devastated areas of the world.

These kinds of gatherings are very important for the Amish communities, underscoring once again the need for interdependency and communal support in all aspects of life along with the requirement that we give generously and with humility of our skills and time.

The frolics also have a lively social aspect to them, being a time when far-flung neighbors can exchange news and gossip, break bread together, and provide a playtime gathering for their many young children. At the same time it is an important opportunity for young folk to see their elders working together, modeling the community interdependency that will become the mainstay of their own lives in Amish culture. Here are demonstrated the practical skills, also, of homemaking or building or farming that all children will need to acquire, and it can be done in a stress-free and enjoyable environment.

No frolic is complete, of course, without food. At the small quiltings and frolics there are always snacks and beverages but it is at the big building frolics such as the barn-raisings that the real food shows up! Every woman and girl in the community will turn out breads, pastries, casseroles, fried chicken, vegetable dishes, and beverages of all kind, and all will sit down to eat at long trestle tables set up under shade trees or in open sheds for just this need, often borrowed from the "church wagon" which hauls benches and tables around the community on alternate Sundays throughout the year.

The men and boys will eat first so as to more quickly return to the large tasks that still await them after the midday meal; the women and girls will take their meals next, and proceed to the long washing-up.

Frolics are a time of family and community, and are an indispensable part of Amish life. Lacking the severity and solemness of Sunday church, these gatherings are the very essence of Amish life as individuals working together toward self-sufficiency, common goals, and common values.

CHAPTER FOUR

Farmhouse

"He has showed thee, O man, what is good, and what the
Lord doth require of thee..."
- Micah 6:8

The Amish farmstead is the most obvious symbol of the *plain*
life that the Amish seek and work so hard to maintain.

Stripped as they are of most—if not all—of the architectural
variety and ornamentation that is the hallmark of that most
cherished of American possessions— the family home—the
Amish farm is distinctive for its conformity to the *Ordnung*,
the rules of the Amish church as they are understood in that
community.

Thus, Amish farmsteads look remarkably alike in their stark
simplicity and so can be easily discerned from among their English neighbors by understanding exactly what it is that makes the
Amish farm unique in the larger American agricultural landscape.

True, some of these differences would seem obvious: the
absence of electrical wiring on the property; a sturdy windmill; a buggy in the yard.

Appearances can fool the eye. An Amish farmstead pur-
chased from an English owner a full year before may still have

the electric wire strung between road and house, house and barn, barn and yardlights—but the electricity was never turned on. Indeed, in more recently established Amish settlements the decision to keep electrical wiring intact is a practical move: the family wants to see how they feel about their new home community and need the farmstead to be easily resaleable if necessary.

Many new young farm families may wait until there is sufficient and steady income from crops or livestock before spending the money to order and erect one of the large windmills, and instead may rely for a time on a gasoline engine to pump water.

Many Amish farmsteads also house workshops or lumberyards that do business with the larger world, and so it is not infrequent to find English automobiles and pickup trucks in the farmyards during the daylight hours. There are some sure signs to look for to indicate whether or not this might be an Amish farm:

Are there banners or flags on the property? The Amish do not permit such displays.

Is there a modern garage? There is no need to house motor vehicles on the Amish farm.

Are there brightly colored plastic swing-sets and toys in the yard? The Amish make their own wood toys and play sets for their children.

Is there a smaller one-story house just to the side of, or attached to, the two-story main house? This is a *dawdy haus* (daw'-dee howz)—literally the "grandfather house"—where often the older generation of the family live when they have given the farm to one of their children and have retired from a life of active farming.

Are there buggy tracks in gravel or snow coming and going from the drive? You very likely have an Amish neighbor there.

Reflecting on the 'Amishness' of a farmstead is greatly simplified when the traveler is among the Upper Midwest's most conservative Amish, the *Swartzentruber*. Kalona's Amish are Old Order Amish and so do not have the strictness about appearance that the Swartzentruber have.

In Kalona you will find brick used in building, gables on the upper stories, wrought iron railings on porches, shutters on the windows, flower baskets hanging from the verandas, and cupolas on the schoolhouses. Though it was unacceptable in our own community, you may even find that the traditional plain brick silo favored by the Amish has been supplanted by the modern blue 'Harvestore' silos that now dot the Upper Midwest farmlands of the English.

The Swartzentruber Amish eschew all such simple ornamentation as not *plain*, and so their farms take on the purity of appearance that is most appealing to the English visitor. Here we will find the tall white wooden houses, built with an L-wing and a broad open wood-railed porch with wooden steps. Here are the unvarying six-pane overhung windows, without shutters. The outbuildings are also plain frame, wooden, and usually white, with red barns. The mailboxes are unfailingly classic black metal, with careful hand-lettered block print indicating the family name in white paint. It is the Swartzentruber, in particular among the national Amish community, who are most likely to recycle building materials gleaned from other sources and so it is very common to see among their farmsteads entire structures going up which clearly reflect materials scrounged from elsewhere.

So it is that in the Old Order communities like Kalona you may need to look a bit more closely to ensure that, indeed, you have found an Amish farm. In the Swartzentruber communities you know without question that you are among the Amish the minute you see one of their classic ultra-plain farmsteads with identical farmsteads lying just across the hundred-acre fields in any direction.

Of course the simplest signposts to your entrance into an Amish community are the many hand-lettered signs on post or rail indicating that crafts and foods are available to English visitors, always ending with the message "No Sunday Sales."

The Plain Life in Detail

The simplicity of the life of the Amish on their farmsteads is very much in the sum of its parts. Being plain is all of a piece: just as the clothing of the Amish is of the most practical design and limited range of color, so is the range and type of building and equipment defined by a chosen conformity to what is proper, plain, and in accord with the *Ordnung*.

Little if any modern farming machinery will be found in field or barn, though small-engine machinery is frequently adapted using a gasoline engine in barns and wash houses. Cows are milked by hand, though sold milk is taken away in gleaming stainless steel trucks driven by the English. Chickens are fed and allowed to roam freely inside and outside of the simple wood henhouse. Pigs lie about freely, raising their young in their loose pens. The great draft horses stand in stall next to their thoroughbred neighbors, their classic heavy leather tack hanging on the nail-post by the stall door, free of ornament or ribbon or gold medallion.

Washing machines, unless run by small engines using gasoline, are hand operated, as are the wringers. Clothing is pegged out to dry in any season and, when taken in, pressed using gasoline irons or the more traditional flatirons heated on the stove. Dishes and cookwear are washed and dried by hand. Food is cooked and baked using wood-fired stoves or, in some communities, on an oil or gas stove. Icehouses employing great blocks of ice covered in sawdust will be used to keep foods and dairy goods.

There certainly are some exceptions to the norm: In some of the more liberal Amish communities one can see Amish farmers driving tractors in the fields but the wheels are steel, not rubber, and so the tractor can never be used for transportation on the township roads. In these same communities you may also see gasoline-powered refrigerators in the kitchens or in a lean-to off the main dining room for the storage of food.

It is in the interior home space of the family that the concept of plain living can be shown most clearly. Here are the plain wood floors and softly painted walls (the Swartzentruber will only use white paint). Rooms contain the minimum of furniture and though many of the handmade pieces are solid and comfortable, they are spartan in design and color. In the more conservative Amish homes you can find calendars on the wall but they will have no attached pictures or images, and no mirrors at any time (in our Old Order home we had a few mirrors). A modest number of books are kept in small bookcases. A hand-wound mantel clock is common.

One spot of color in an Amish house may be the half-window curtains, in the more conservative communities just simple hemmed lengths strung along braces of wire above the window frame, usually of soft colors that match the room décor. The Swartzentruber have been known to put up deep blue curtains in the front lower windows to indicate that there is a marriage-age girl in the family.

In the upstairs bedrooms clothing is hung on pegs along the wall or in simple open closets or freestanding wardrobes. Wash basins and bowls are placed on dresser tops for water that is drawn from the hand-pump at the kitchen sink (some of the more liberal Amish communities do permit indoor bathrooms). Simple coverlets and quilts are draped over the beds. All rooms are in neatness. No space is wasted; most Amish houses are built above a deep foundation, and it is in the cool lower basement rooms with their cement floors that we would see hundreds of gleaming glass jars showing the canning efforts from gardening and butchering. Here also are stored eggs, and bulk bags of flour and sugar kept in tight bins off the floor.

The Millers at Home

My family lived an Old Order life as did most of our Kalona community. This meant that we observed the church rules, the *Ordnung*, on what was permitted and what was not and though we did embrace some modern conveniences—mostly in the form of gas-powered small engines to run some utilities—we nevertheless accepted and lived a plain life.

We had an 80-acre farm with a large white barn along with several other white outbuildings. The corncrib was the building where a few wagons and our steel-wheeled tractor were kept. There was a grain elevator in the center of the building that took grain to the bins along the walls and also to bins located in the top half of the building. The chicken house was on one side of this building next to an area where the sows were fed. We had several hog sheds equipped to accommodate the sows with their little ones and large feeding areas where pigs were fattened for market.

There was also a rain shelter and a free-standing chicken house with a fenced in area where the chickens or fryers being fattened could go outside to feed. Near the corn crib stood an old building with a shop area in one corner and room to store some field equipment and a couple buggies.

Later as the family grew and needed more buggies, a large building was erected close to the house. It consisted of a wash house, a large area to store the buggies, machinery, and field equipment, and a large shop area where my brother Elson welded and repaired buggy wheels. Behind this shed stood our wood house formerly used as an icehouse.

Our home was a wooden white-framed 3-1/2 story house, structured with a basement, main floor, upstairs and attic. My parent's bedroom was on the main floor, and there were four bedrooms upstairs for us children and for guests.

The kitchen had a pantry, gas refrigerator and oven, and counters along the walls with plenty of cabinets above and below. The dining room had a built-in china cabinet for our best dishes and next to it was a large table surrounded with chairs. The living room had plain furniture: a hickory bent rocker, two plain upholstered couches, an old-fashioned recliner, and an oak desk.

The bedrooms were furnished very simply, with just a bed and an oak dresser in each. Most of our beds were the old-fashioned kind with the open coil springs. Our bedrooms were similar to our parents' and the floors throughout the house were all linoleum. Before the addition was put onto our house, the living room had a hardwood floor.

In 1989, when I was fifteen, we put on an additional ten feet to the west side of the house giving us quite a bit more room and an upstairs bathroom. Before that we only had one bathroom with a bathtub on the main floor for the entire family, and relied on the outhouse as a back-up. We had running water, so we didn't have a pump at the sink.

The *dawdy haus* that was attached to the main house did have a pump at the sink. A widow lived in the *dawdy haus* but she died when I was still quite small. I remember my siblings and I taking food to her sometimes and I know she shared a lot of advice and good home remedies with my parents. Today it has been completely remodeled and my brother Benedict's family lives in it.

Our windmill pumped our drinking water into a holding tank that was inside a white building just next to it. Rainwater was channeled by gutters into a cistern under the house where it was pumped into a pressurized tank for our running water. We had a gas water heater in the basement for hot water, and our gas refrigerator and oven were all fueled by a propane gas tank behind the house.

Along the Roadside

The Amish are the original organic farmers and original recyclers. It is a tenet of their belief, as Christians practicing the way of life that God wishes for them, that they not despoil the earth, and that they use what they have at hand and not ask for more. It is true that, in the later 20th century, many Amish experimented with chemicals in the fields but it is fading as an acceptable idea.

A great many Amish farmers in the Upper Midwest now partake regularly in regional produce markets and many are now offering organic products. Though we do not participate in government farm programs or standards systems, in many districts the Amish farmers are creating their own organic certification standards which parallel the national organic standards that were set by the U.S. Food and Drug Administration. In this way the Amish farmer can sell to buyers seeking certified organic produce and can also reasonably compete with other organic growers in an ever-competitive agricultural market.

Beyond caring for the soil, the Amish have always maintained a reverence for nature as a part of God's divine creation. Woods and meadows are carefully fostered, as are fencings and roadside ditches, and great care is taken to never despoil the beauty of the land for short term gain. It is a peace the Amish communities seek in partnership with the natural world that helps them always to remember their place in God's world.

Perhaps most poignant and clear a reminder of this simplicity of life can be found in the perfume of wood smoke that is an ever-present aspect of life in the midst of Amish farmlands.

Drifting from woodstove and smokehouse, brush-pile and campfire, the pungent and unmistakable smoky scent wafting over field and road reminds passersby that, in any season and dawn or dusk, they are in a unique and sheltered world, its boundaries clear and its rules set.

CHAPTER FIVE

Schoolhouse

For wisdom of the world is foolishness with God.
- I Cor 3:19

Life in the Amish home and the Amish school is intimately related, each providing the support the child needs to gain skills for living a life in the Amish church community and for interaction with the English world beyond.

At home Amish children learn their place in the family, the ways in which they are expected to accept responsibility with humility. At school they are given the tools they will need to participate—within the limits of the *Ordnung*— with the larger world of the English while still fully immersed in the world of Amish ways.

In the 1970s the United States Government recognized the right of Amish communities to establish their own schools apart from the English education system. Before that time, Amish children attended rural one-room and consolidated schools with their English and Mennonite neighbors, and the strain on the Amish community to maintain a plain life in the midst of an increasingly sophisticated and technical English society was growing every decade.

The landmark case of Wisconsin vs. Yoder was an argument between the Amish and the United States government over a law which stated that all children must attend public school until the age of sixteen. The Amish families being represented refused to obey this law and took their children out of school after the 8th grade with the stated belief that high school attendance went against their religious beliefs.

The State of Wisconsin challenged this case in the United States Supreme Court, which brought down a decision in May 1972 on behalf of the national Amish community, citing a basic constitutional right to the freedom of religion.

So, just as many mainstream American church communities have established their parochial schools, so did the Amish petition for recognition as a distinct religious minority. Agreeing to maintain American education standards from grades 1-8, the Amish communities around the nation quickly moved to build their own one-room schoolhouses, and have continued to do so into the 21st century. Children remain in school until the 8th grade, generally around the age of 14, at which time they may return to be of help in the family farming endeavors or find acceptable employment in the nearby community, contributing their wages to the family. Schooling beyond the 8th grade would not, the Amish believe, be fit for a rural agricultural Christian people, and could only lead to pride.

The One-Room Schoolhouse

The general population of any Amish community can be estimated by counting the number of one-room schoolhouses dotting a community of Amish farms, a general count of 20-35 children being accommodated in any one Amish school. As of Autumn 2003 there were ten schools (including a school for 'special children') in the Kalona community, an indication of the considerable size of the Kalona (Johnson/Washington County) Amish community, the first independent school being built in 1966 and the most recent in 2000.

Kalona is not unusual in this size of Amish population for the Upper Midwest, being matched by the Bloomfield Amish settlement in Iowa's Davis County, the Harmony-Canton Amish community in Minnesota's Fillmore County, and the Wilton Amish community in Wisconsin's Monroe County.

These districts are dwarfed by the exceptional size of the Cashton Amish community in Wisconsin's Vernon/Monroe County region: here an astonishing twenty-three schoolhouses have been built since 1966, jumping in number each decade as an indication of the increasing number of families having children who are growing up in, or have moved into, the district. Nor is the pace abating: just since 1999, six new schools have been built to accommodate a probable count of 150 additional school-age Amish children in the Cashton area.

The traditional Amish one-room school will have two front-facing doors—one for the boys, and one for the girls—as well as a cloakroom, a small closet, and a basement area. Traditional all-of-a-piece wood desks face the front blackboard and the teacher's desk. Long benches range against the back wall for frequent visitors: parents, student teachers, the schoolboard elders. A large freestanding wood cabinet holds books and supplies: pencils, ruled paper pads and ledgerbooks, chalk and erasers for the board. A wood-burning stove provides heat and a place to warm winter soups and cocoa. Light is provided from the range of windows along one wall, and sometimes by a skylight.

Traditional wooden privies—again, one for the boys and one for the girls—are found at the back of the yard, sometimes shielded by shrubs or bushes. A hitching post is usually found near the front doors. Cords of wood are stacked near a side door, which opens onto a small recreation field where softball and jumprope and other children's games are played. Sometimes there is a small outbuilding at the back where tools and other maintenance supplies can be stored.

Amish schools—like Amish cemeteries—are almost always to be found on a small parcel of farmland belonging to one of the community's farmers, and the families of school age children look after the grounds and the building. Guidance for the school is taken up by a board of elders who interview and hire the teacher (or teachers, in the instance of a larger student population), arrange for firewood, approve alterations to and maintenance of the schoolhouse, budget for the purchase of teaching supplies, and oversee the curriculum planning. They approve the textbooks and make recommendations on questions of religious teachings and the *Ordnung*.

The teachers hired by the school's board of elders have frequently grown up in the community and may well know most if not all of the families who are sending their children to school. The training of these young teachers—traditionally mostly young unmarried women but also more young men as the number of Amish schools continues to grow rapidly—is built upon their own 8th-grade education with summer learning meetings where teachers from many communities will gather to receive general training for the classroom. Amish teachers may begin teaching as early as age 17.

The school board elders themselves are frequent visitors to the school, as are the children's' parents and often also the ministers and bishop of the district, bringing a direct quality of homeliness, sacredness and caring to the Amish learning environment. Thus it is that Amish children are never asked to make an intellectual or emotional break between what is learned at home, at school, or at worship.

As with Amish Old Order and Swartzentruber farmstead architecture, there are real differences between Old Order and Swartzentruber schoolhouses. Old Order Amish schoolhouses can be found of many building materials, commonly white-painted wood but just as often of brick. They almost always have a bell tower or cupola atop the schoolhouse. Many Old Order schools are also seen to have deep porches running along the front of the building and can also be found with shutters.

In contrast, Swartzentruber Amish schools seldom stray from a basic style: white-painted wood, double six-pane windows without shutters, no bell tower or cupola, no porch. The school bell hangs instead from a pole near the front doors and is rung by a short handrope. Swartzentruber Amish schools are entirely uniform in appearance: variation would be seen as extremely unusual.

Off to School

Every Amish child makes their first journey from home to school around the age of six or seven. Now they are "scholars," as the Amish fondly call their school-aged children.

They leave the world of family and familiarity and, in the company of siblings and the children of their neighbors, they enter the world of abstractions—words, numbers, and concepts—the same that are shared in a superficial way with English children in America but are, beneath the surface, moving Amish children toward significantly different goals.

They will stay until the age of fourteen at which time they will return to their family life year round, becoming part of the working rhythm of house and farm.

The older school-age children ("scholars") in Amish families set the pattern that all their siblings will follow: from September to May they are up at dawn to help with kitchen and farm chores, then a big farm breakfast, and the getting ready for school.

The hair of the younger girls is braided, and they will wear a girl's traditional garb of a long under-dress, a back-buttoned apron (what the English would call a pinafore), dark hose and dark shoes. They will wear deep black felted bonnets in winter, and perhaps a scarf in summer. A long cape-like shawl will cover them in the cold.

The boys—younger and older— are wearing dark pants, solid color shirts and suspenders, black boots, and the necessary hat: black felt in winter, straw in summer. Short jackets will keep them warm in the cold.

The older girls are now dressing much the way their mothers dress, their attire making the most dramatic change. Gone are the pinafores and the braids. In their place are the full dress and apron of solid color—fastened with straight pins—and the long hair is now coiled at the back of the neck and almost wholly covered with a white prayer cap. Black stockings and black shoes complete the wardrobe, with the black bonnet and shawl worn in colder weather.

When its time to depart for school the children's mother will give each of the children a lunch pail or bag, or a large basket with lunch for all of the children in the family, to be shared out by the eldest sibling. Then the children will walk down the farmstead drive to the road and join other neighbor children if the school is nearby; or, if the schoolhouse is farther away, or the weather is severe, their father or an older sibling will hitch up a wagon and the children will be driven to school, to be picked up at the end of the afternoon.

Once at school, the pattern of learning never varies: the teacher will work with each child, in groups or individually, according to the grade level they have reached that year. The older scholars will frequently help tutor the younger students. All of the expected learning tasks can be found in the Amish school: reading, writing and grammar, working with numbers, all framed against the standards of the American educational system for grades 1-8. Tests are given, writing assignments are given out, mathematical problems are worked at the board. A globe will help Amish children, living as they do in a culture that seeks separation from the world, to understand something of the world's geography.

English is always used for teaching at school. Amish scholars begin learning English at a very young age, as is entirely necessary for life that works with and around the 'English' as a neighboring culture. Thus, Amish children are solidly bilingual by their early teens, a claim that would be nearly impossible for most American children to make.

It is important to understand that Amish learning is not for its own sake. Amish culture has virtually no intellectual goals, but rather learned skills are tools for reinvestment in Amish life, the Amish church, the needs of the community as understood in the *Ordnung* and in the Bible. Learning humility before God, submission to the *Ordnung* and the great community good, and accepting a plain life as befits a plain people are the sole aim of all Amish life.

Reading and writing, as taught in the Amish school, are needed for ease of communication and business interaction with the larger world of the English, but the overriding desire is to be able to read prayers, and religious and faith-based books and stories.

The manual skills taught at home, which are needed to maintain daily life, promote the work that is pleasing to God and that falls within the *Ordnung*: farming, and woodworking, the craft of Jesus and his family.

Early School Days in Kalona

There were eight Amish schools in Kalona when I was growing up. Because we lived pretty much in the middle of the community, the school I attended was called Centerville School; the other schools were Shady Lane, Friendship, Pleasant Valley, Middleburg, Sunny Slope, Maple Grove, and Glenbrook. The community started a school by the name of HOPE around 1996, standing for *Handicapped Oriented Parochial Education*.

The school is for our "special children," being the deaf, the retarded, or those with severe physical disabilities. A tenth school, Echo Vale, was built in 2000 after I had already left Kalona.

I started kindergarten when I was six years old, which is the usual age. Kindergarten is only several days a week for several weeks in the spring before school ends for the year.

When school started back up the following August I started first grade and went every day. The first day of school, I was so excited as I walked the quarter mile with my siblings and the neighbor children that walked with us as they passed our place on their way to school. My brothers and I usually walked the quarter mile to school every day. We were only driven to school by buggy when it was raining or it was *really* cold. I remember walking to school many times and our legs would be numb with cold by the time we got there.

We spoke Pennsylvania Dutch, or *Deutsche*, until we got to school at which time we were supposed to speak English. I had two classmates and we couldn't speak English very well but we could understand most of it and being around it all day helped us learn it faster. (I learned English faster when my parents and older siblings spoke English when they said something they didn't want me to understand!)

The one-room schoolhouse I attended had two entrances, one that led to the basement and the other to the classroom. When you entered the front door, a small flight of stairs led to the classroom and to the right a flight of stairs led to the basement. Next to the stairs that led to the basement, was the boys' cloakroom and restroom. The girls' was to the left of the front entrance. Because our community allowed indoor plumbing, we didn't have outhouses at school. The cloakrooms were full of hooks for our bonnets, hats, and winter wraps along with shelves for our lunch buckets.

The classroom was filled with desks in neat rows and the front of the room had a large blackboard, teacher's desk, and a table and bench for classes. In the back of the room was the library where the dictionaries and encyclopedia set were kept. Windows lined each side of the classroom for plenty of light and there were bulletin boards for decorations. On one of the walls was a visitor's bench. We had one or two teachers depending on the number of students and they taught all eight grades.

On a typical school day the teacher would begin with roll call and then read us a Bible story. We would sing two songs and recite our weekly Bible verse. This would be followed with a prayer, most often the Lord's Prayer recited in English, and only occasionally in German. German was the language of home, and English was the language of school, which greatly enhanced fluency.

Our class study topics were very much like any English school room around the country: English, arithmetic, social studies, reading and vocabulary work, writing and spelling. We also had some basic health and art classes, and the older children would have a limited amount of science studies also. My favorite studies were English and spelling and I won my fair share of spelling bees over the years.

The lunches we brought from home in our buckets were always delicious and filling. We'd usually find egg, bologna or cheese sandwiches on home-made bread, a container of fresh or canned fruit, and a portion of cake or maybe cookies. My mother would make wonderful fruit cobblers for supper and we'd usually find the leftovers tucked into our lunchpails the next day. In the winter we'd bring soup to leave on the top of the kerosene stove in the basement so that it was nice and warm by lunchtime. Even more fun, we'd sometimes bring a container of ice cream and bury it in the snow to keep it frozen!

Lunchtime was forty-five minutes, and we had fifteen-minute breaks at mid-morning and mid-afternoon. As good as the food was in our lunchpails, we didn't waste a lot of time eating because this was when we'd all dash out to play games in the schoolyard. We played running games at recess when the weather was cold but our favorite sport when the weather permitted was softball. I was very competitive and I relished watching the boys back up in the outfield when I came up to bat or hitting the ball over the fence to make a home run!

We were expected to do our work in school and only had homework if we got sick or fell behind. Falling behind was frowned upon because we had chores at home we were expected to do. Minor offences in the schoolroom or schoolyard were usually punished by having the child stand with their nose in a corner (or centered on a circle drawn on the blackboard). For less grievous offences, we would be expected to stay in during recess and sweep the floor, or stay after school for other modest maintenance duties.

A spanking would only be meted out for something truly

egregious, and woe be to the scholar who merited such harsh punishment as it would surely be duplicated in exact form upon reaching home!

I went to the same school all through my school years and there were 18-25 students during this time.

I finished school at age fourteen and I was thrilled. Even though I enjoyed school a lot, education wasn't a priority for me in those years. I wanted to be home doing all the things that seemed a lot more fun than school.

School and the Amish Year

Younger children in Amish families know that, someday, they too will climb into the horse-drawn wagon or, taking the hands of their older siblings, walk down the road to their one-room schoolhouse and walk into the world of learning. They will become scholars.

And for the next nine or ten years they will learn to balance the expectations of their parents, their teachers and their communities, bowing and bending to the rhythm of home, farm, classroom and the church community.

That all these distinct places are intricately interlinked in Amish life may not become consciously evident in a child's mind until they are in their mid-teens, at which time great change—long in accruing—comes to all young Amish people as they ready themselves to take their place as adults in their separate world of plain people.

To this end, Amish life spins Sunday to Sunday, from house to farm, to school, and then to church again on Sunday, God's

Sabbath, the day of community worship and study. Children in Amish life are prepared for this Seventh Day through the prayers they are learning in school, the Bible chapters heard and the Bible verses recited there, the visits from the Bishop and the small homilies that the ministers may give. The Amish School is, for these children, not a place and activity separate from Sunday worship but truly a lead-in to Sunday worship, bringing the wheel of the seasons and the year around to God and the *Ordnung* every seven days.

CHAPTER SIX

No Sunday Sales

The Lord of Heaven and Earth dwelleth not
in the temples made with hands.
- Acts 17:24

To be Amish is to be Christian, to live as Christ and the first Christians lived. All life is to be in simplicity, communality, and humility.

From Sunday to Sunday the Amish community life returns to its primary roots in traditions of Christian worship that are repeated in hundreds of Amish house churches throughout the United States. Exactly what is read, and said, and sung at each community's Sunday worship may vary somewhat depending on that community's *Ordnung*, the unwritten code of laws that govern life in the community, but the essence and appearance of Sunday worship and conduct would be recognized as Amish anywhere in the country.

The Bible provides the foundation for Amish Sunday worship, advising the community to hold church services in the home, and to submit to the *Ordnung* and to the elders of the church ("Likewise, ye younger, submit yourselves unto the elders. Yea, all of you be subject to one another." I Peter 5:5).

No business or commerce of any kind may take place on a Sunday, thus the common phrase found beneath many Amish community roadside shop signs "No Sunday Sales."

"...Not In The Temples Made With Hands."

A single Amish church is devised of a district with as many as 30 or more families, and for each district there are several ministers, a deacon, and a bishop. A large community such as Cashton, Wisconsin may have a great many church districts.

As the early church was known to have followed the dictate of the New Testament in Acts by drawing lots, so too do the Amish church congregants observe their nominees for minister and bishop drawing lots before the assembly. "...And they gave forth their lots, and the lot fell to Matthias..." (Acts 1:26)

Those men elected serve for life wherever they may find themselves in the years to come, without any other compensation than that which comes knowing that God has asked him to preach His word to the assembled and to watch over the church community as would any shepherd with his flock.

Within each church district, as within each family, boys and girls, and men and women, fulfill their understood roles as expressed in the Bible and acknowledged through the *Ordnung*. In partnership, biblical law and Amish societal law weave a tight fabric of expectations and implications for the life of the individual within the community.

A church district meets on alternating Sundays in family homes on a rotational basis throughout the district. Most Amish church districts meet as a "house church:" only the most liberal

Amish communities meet, as do their Mennonite neighbors, in specially built structures called 'churches.'

If the family house is large enough, doors can be folded or slid back to open up the entire first floor to permit the placement of the long backless church benches that are carried about the church district on the 'bench wagon' for delivery to the next house church location.

If a family house is more modest, the barn or a large workshop or shed is swept and readied for the congregation; on pleasant weather days the barn doors are left open to permit fresh air and sunlight to filter in during the three or more hours of worship.

The families have gathered by midmorning, many arriving by buggy where men and boys will unhitch and lead away the horses to be looked after through the long hours ahead while the buggies remain in long lines in the yard. Some families who live nearby will set out to walk together down the road to the neighboring farm where church worship will take place. Everyone is in their best clothing, dark suits and hats and fresh white shirts for the men and boys; colored dresses, white organdy aprons and black headcoverings on the girls and unmarried women; and colored dresses, matching capes and aprons and white organdy *kapps* for the married women.

Once inside the house or barn where church services are to be held, the men and boys sort themselves out to one side, the girls and women the other side. Children under the age of three will sit with either parent; girl children under the age of eleven will sit with their mothers, the boys with their fathers. Coats and cloaks and bonnets will be hung in the basement or in a separate area of the house. Women will often be seated nearest the doors to the kitchen (or to the yard) so as to be available for meal preparation and serving, or to look after their youngsters.

The most noticeable aspect of Amish church services is language: the Amish will speak English at school and in the outside world, and *Deutsche* in the home, but in worship they use the medieval High German only, reading out the scriptures from an approved High German translation of the King James Bible, reciting prayers from the German prayerbook known as the *Christenpflicht*, (kree'-sten-fleekt), and singing in the long, minor-key hymnody of the *Ausbund* (owz'-boond) or the *Lieder Sammelung* (lee'-dur sam'-ah-loong), the Amish hymnbooks.

High German is to the Amish as Latin once was to Catholic life before Vatican II: an ancient language used for the holiness of worship with the element of the mysterious, the unknown to those who do not regularly converse in such a language. So it is that the Amish reserve High German only for Sundays, and must learn both the pronunciations and translations by memory, entirely reliant upon the elders for interpretation which can vary substantially from district to district, and region to region.

The church district looks to its ordained for direction in the worship service and for the Word as inspired by God through these elders. The district's bishop is the final word on issues of interpretation and application of the Holy Scriptures and the *Ordnung*. It is the bishop who will perform the holy sacraments of baptism, wedding, and funeral. The district ministers are the preachers to the community and will speak once or severally during the many hours of house church worship. The deacon's role is both logistical, assuring that all is in preparation for the Sunday worship, and ecclesiastical, often being called upon to read scriptural passages. The deacon is also the first line of defense of the *Ordnung*, being watchful in the community for trespassing of the accepted rule of Amish life in that district.

At the conclusion of the service the assembled district congregation partakes of the Sunday noon meal together. ("When ye come together to eat, tarry one for another." I Cor. 11:33) Men and boys are seated first at the same long benches used earlier in the worship service and now moved to match long plank tables set up on sawhorses. They are served by the women and girls who have been busy preparing the traditional meal of sliced bread, jams, jellies, peanut butter, pickled beets and cucumbers, and tea and coffee. It is a meal easily assembled and served, and without overwhelming expense for the hosting family.

When the men and boys have cleared their plates, the women and girls will sit for their repast and then retire to the washhouse or kitchen to perform the clean-up duties while the menfolk talk farming and family news. Everyone then departs as they came, matching up their horses to their buggies and heading down the farm drive in a great long line, followed by the families who had arrived on foot.

In-Between Sundays

The alternate Sundays between district house church gatherings are spent at home with family reading from scripture and devotional material. Families in some communities meet for Sunday School to study the Bible and children memorize German hymns, prayers and Bible verses.

The day will pass among family and, though normal family and farm chores must be done, no major tasks or projects are undertaken on Sundays. Instead, it is a day of much visiting among friends and family members, and a day of service to those who are alone, ill or in need. Sundays are the day of the week that the English will see the greatest number of the distinctive Amish buggies on the road going to and from other farms for long visits.

A Miller Family Sunday

Sunday chores and breakfast were like any other day for our family but we moved about in a hurry to ensure getting to church on time.

While we women and girls washed the dishes after breakfast, the men and boys went out to groom the horses and hitch them to the clean buggies which had been washed the day before in preparation.

Young people didn't have to be there as early as the ministers so my brother Elson and sister Bertha would often come later in the single buggy, while the rest of us rode in the larger surrey with our parents. (When Elson got his own buggy at 21, Wilbur and Benedict used the single buggy.)

The way I dressed for church as a little girl was in a button-down dress that closed in the back and instead of wearing the usual apron that matches it, I wore a white starched organdy apron over the dress with a black head covering.

Once I had reached the age of eleven, my dress closed in the front with straight pins and I wore a white starched organdy cape and apron over my colored dress, along with a black head covering like all the unmarried girls. Mom would fix and pin my sister's cape before Dad was ready to go, and then Mom or Bertha would pin mine.

For Sunday the boys were dressed in white shirts with navy or black pants along with a matching coat for winter and vest in the summer. When we got to church, I followed my mother to the basement or part of the house where the bonnets and wraps were kept.

The married women greeted each other with a handshake and the Holy Kiss before making their way to where the service was to begin. Men did the same with each other before coming to the house. I waited with the other girls as more people arrived and more girls joined our group. All the girls that didn't sit with their mothers waited to file into church shortly before it was to begin and again the same with the boys.

The women with small babies sat in one room and the rest sat in the room facing the men. The girls filed to the front of the women's room and the boys to the front of the men's room.

Church always began at 9:30 A.M. and the service was opened with a song from the *German Lieder Sammlung*. On the second line the bishop and ministers filed upstairs to take council with each other. The second hymn sung was always the *Lob Lied* (lobe leed)—literally, the *praise song*—and if the ministers hadn't returned by the time that song was done we sang others until they got back. The *Lob Lied* alone takes twenty to twenty-five minutes to sing.

The minister who gave the opening sermon would preach for about half an hour, after which everyone knelt while he read a German prayer from the *Christenpflicht*. When the prayer was done, everyone stood while the deacon read a chapter from the Bible.

The second minister preached the 'main part' of the service that lasted perhaps an hour. A plate of cookies and crackers would be passed here for the smaller children to keep them busy; also, though no one was allowed to whisper or talk during this time, the children would use handkerchiefs to make little animals to entertain themselves.

The minister would then read a chapter from the Bible, followed by a few short testimonies from the other ministers in agreement to his sermon. Everyone knelt again as he prayed and, as we stood following this last prayer, he recited a short blessing.

The bishop gave a closing benediction and made any announcements that the community needed to be aware of. The service ended with a final song unless the members had to *still hocka*, (shteel hah'-ka), which means to discuss church problems, or hear someone who needed to make a confession. *Still hocka* is done only after all the children and non-members have gone outside.

Miller Home Sundays

In the summertime, on our in-between Sundays, we gathered at a plain building in the community where we held Sunday School. The Kalona Amish community originates from Somerset, Pennsylvania which has special buildings as church houses, and we likely brought this same tradition to Iowa.

There is one Sunday School building each on the north and south sides of the Kalona Amish community. The south Sunday School building was located across the road from the back edge of our family's property, so we children almost always walked for the service.

There were eight church districts in the Kalona Amish community, so two districts of the south part of the community had house church while the other two held Sunday School. The same pattern endured for the north part of the community. The following Sunday the two Sunday School buildings were used for the four districts that had church the Sunday before.

In the wintertime we didn't have Sunday School but for six weeks the Sunday School building was used for German School or " Dutch (*Deutsche*) College." German School was for those of us who were done with grade school and we read, wrote, and spelled in German. Every week during this time the whole community of young people would attend a spelling bee held in someone's home. I won a few of these as well as some in grade school. I just loved spelling!

When we didn't have Sunday School, the day was spent at home unless we went to our friends' house in other districts for church. Since my dad was a minister, my parents went to other districts for church a lot instead of staying home.

If the whole family was home on such a day, my dad would pick out some chapters in the Bible and everyone took turns reading a verse until the chapter ended. We would also sing a few songs. After that everyone could pretty much do as they pleased, such as playing board games, reading, or catching up on some much-needed sleep.

Sundays were to be spent with the least amount of physical labor possible, allowing only the things that had to be done, such as cooking and choring. No money was to be exchanged on this day. We were allowed to play some games but none that required a lot of activity.

Church Sunday or not, most Sunday afternoons were spent visiting old people or families with a new baby or perhaps someone that needed cheering after some misfortune.

Veiled in Mystery

Amish life, being both patriarchal and based on the literal and revealed Word of the Bible, fosters separation from the world. Life lived according to the scripture of the Bible is the very essence of any Amish community. Thus, submission to the Word of God, as it is interpreted and conveyed by the men who serve as elders, is key to the stable continuation of Amish culture.

The Word of God as it is read and spoken in the ancient language of High German is a greatly complicating factor in the religious life of the individual in any Amish community, and it is the necessity for an individual's submission to the interpretations and explanations by the elders that allows for smooth continuity. Individual interpretation or philosophical soul-searching beyond the boundaries of the accepted interpretation by Amish elders of the church is greatly discouraged, for it could only lead to questions...and then to change.

Yet questions arise, and change does come. The remarkably high mobility of Amish families, both from community to community and from region to region, displays the recurrent issues of concern over matters of interpretation for both worship and community law.

A church district can, and often does, offer an alternative on an acceptable understanding of Biblical teachings and the governing *Ordnung* of a community. Those who seek a more liberal, or more stringent, approach will find it if they search, and many do, often traveling great distances to set down roots once again in another Amish community which may accept a broader questioning and a great sense of individuality, or quashes both more thoroughly.

The peace and community solidarity of the Amish Sunday worship does not always bring the solace of heart and soul that is sought, and for those who continue to question, and thence to suffer, the sense of being 'other' in a world of those who have submitted in humility can take root when still young and continue to make its presence known in the passages from youth to adulthood.

A life alive in Christ, doing the complete bidding of God, in full humility and *gelassenheit* (submission) according to His Word, is the daily hope of every Amish man and woman. It is in our collective human nature to seek joy in spirit, and the mobility of the Amish will continue to provide a counterbalance to inflexibility in biblical and social law, allowing those who must ask to find answers to their questions, and finally a place to call Home.

CHAPTER SEVEN

Consider the Lilies

*...that women adorn themselves in modest apparel...not
with plaited hair, or gold or pearls, or costly array.*
1 Timothy 2:39

The time of adolescence is the most challenging for any culture. Bodies are changing, expectations for conduct swirl about
the young in the form of family and church understandings of
conduct and bodily sanctity, and the entirety of the outside
world affects any child in today's world.

For the Amish—a closed, scripture-based, patriarchal society—the mysteries and complexities of being male and female
are clothed in the Word of God, and bounded in by the
Ordnung.

A teaching pamphlet "To A Girl of Eleven" concerning
sexuality, written for Amish and Mennonite girls, ends with a
clear message:

*Cherish your purity, be watchful and earnest, pray fervently,
guard it well, and God will bless you.*

The pamphlet 'To A Boy of Twelve' ends very differently,

exhorting them to step forward to take their place in the world of men.

...[be] obedient, clean, respectful, strong and manly.

The natural turmoil of Amish adolescence is permitted few outlets until the age of sixteen, when an Amish family will acknowledge the tradition of *rumspringe* (room'-shpring-uh)— the "running around time"—and accept that their older teen is going to do some serious exploring of self-identity outside of the Amish community.

But for the younger teens, particularly the girls, there are few of the social outlets that their contemporaries in English life enjoy—for better or for ill—and the pressure of conformity, which provides a fundamental tenet of Amish church life, combined with a strong 'father' culture can create either a truly happy child...or a terribly embattled one.

"Cherish Your Purity..."

Amish boys and girls are taught from their youngest days that the salvation of their souls is greatly dependent on their obedience to the laws of the church, which naturally includes very clear understandings about purity of conduct and expression.

Lessons in the Amish home, in church, and in Sunday School daily underscore their gender roles. The *Ordnung* will provide the boundaries of acceptable comportment in the community. Books may be provided, and scripture lessons given that speak to the natural human dilemmas of maintaining the holiness of the body. There are health classes in school but no direct sexual education classes for the young teens, and so as happens so often for children, what is learned about the body is relayed through whispers and rumors and playground news. This system of learning about the body, about its beauty and its mysteries, is as old as humanity.

If the Amish mother, or older sisters, are able to tell young girls about what is happening to their bodies, a great benefit is accorded the child. But, as happens very often, the descriptions of the body changes, and the information on the nature of sexuality and reproduction, are given couched in the understanding that the purity of the girl's body is hers to guard, and that she must defend against both the pressures of the interests of boys, and against her own natural desires, so as to be a fit and chaste bride for her future husband.

"...Be Watchful And Earnest..."

Swirling around Amish adolescents are the endless reminders of English cultural attitudes toward body, sexuality and social permissiveness.

Any Amish child who walks into a small-town convenience store is immediately confronted with display racks of our magazine covers, movie rentals, newspapers, popular novels and romances, hip-hop music on the store speakers, and the regular appearance of young English teens their own age, with their easy and open body language and their casual clothing.

It is a huge source of confusion in Amish families, long past the age when a child simply asks "Why?" and has moved firmly to "Why not?"

In the early teen years, before the time of *rumspringe,* this inevitable exposure to English culture is firmly, even vehemently, countered with home instruction and church admonitions in the constant battle for the child's mind and soul. Statistics continue to show that most Amish young people do finally accept adult baptism in the tradition of Anabaptist churches, and settle down into the Amish community as an adult. But the passage cannot be simple.

A girl child passes into her teen years with the marker of a change of clothing. The pinafore and the braids disappear, to be replaced with the garb of the unmarried female in Amish society: solid color dress, cape and apron, white muslin pleated *kapp,* dark hose and dark shoes. Only the chosen color of her dress will permit creativity, and even then the choices are greatly limited.

Her young teen years are now split evenly between school and home. School provides a healthy outlet for the young minds, moving in these last three years of classes into the broader subjects of geography, art, writing and basic sciences. Here also are the sandlot games, softball and kickball and volleyball, physical outlets for growing young bodies. Home life continues the modeling of the skills and comportment that are her expected lot in life as an Amish woman, accepted with *gelassenheit* and a willing heart. Dolls and other toys are now often set aside as young girls learn the critical art of household management, care for younger siblings, and help with farm chores.

Young girls will often start to accompany their older sisters and mothers to quiltings or other frolics, taking their place as responsible young women. Handcrafted work often begins in earnest with this age group as an important contribution to family income. The charming baskets, straw weavings, potholders, aprons and conserves which are sold to the English visitors and to shops in town provide an important creative outlet for these girls.

In the midst of this outward cultural shift, girls must confront their changing bodies and the response that comes to these changes from the church community. Anxiety, frustration, confusion and contradiction are often the lot of the Amish teen, with few outlets for the basic information that has become the hallmark of health education for English youngsters. Social stigma, based on the *Ordnung* and scripture, can chase a girl child in real misery her entire adolescence, without recourse to alternatives in body image or emotional health.

"…Pray Fervently…"

There was never any sex education, not for the girls in our family anyway. You learned at an early age not to ask any questions pertaining this matter. One didn't get an answer and was told not to talk about it. A friend in school told me she knew what the word sex meant but refused to tell me. I used the word in scrabble while playing a game at home and Mom sternly told me not to use it again.

Attraction and boyfriend/girlfriend behavior in school was forbidden and was treated as a shameful thing. Even in the young folk circle it's not encouraged to have real 'friends' among the opposite sex, and dating under the age of eighteen was frowned upon.

After I joined the church several boys made confessions in church for *'fleisches list und selbst befleckung.'* Of course I didn't understand what these German phrases stood for, so I asked Mom. She got embarrassed and said she'd rather not say. Since I've left the Amish I've found out these phrases stand for masturbation and other sex sins.

As a young girl, when English men brought their horses to be trained, I would watch as they unloaded their horses from the trailer that was hooked to their fancy trucks. They wore fascinating but strange clothes and some of their horses looked strange too, being show horses with bobbed or braided tails.

I would also stand around to watch when other English men came such as the feedman, veterinarian, or someone to pick up cattle. There were times when the veterinarian came, I would be sent to the house without an explanation regardless if I asked for one. I would listen to their conversations with my dad and brothers and I would hear phrases like 'in heat' or when referring to a stallion, "His attitude needs to be adjusted."

Anytime there was a birth among the farm animals the boys went out to help, but we girls were to stay in the house and I'm sure they also helped with the breeding. When the men 'worked with the pigs' or when my uncle came to 'work on the horses' we were informed not to come to the barn.

I remember Mom coming home from town one day and I spotted "maxi pads." She seemed uncomfortable when I asked her what they were and said she'd tell me later when I got older.

When I was eleven or twelve, she explained what the pads were for and briefly explained that a period is something that happens to a girl every month. She showed me where she hid the pads and how the used ones were to be wrapped in magazine pages to make them look like 'regular' trash. She told me not to talk to the boys (my brothers) about this because they were not to know anything about it.

She also gave me a little booklet to read that she had borrowed from our neighbor called "For a Girl of Eleven." It stated in very general clinical terms how the female anatomy worked and one section caught my attention but I knew I was not to ask about it. It briefly stated that if a woman lays with a man a certain way, the egg would be fertilized, she'd get pregnant, and a baby would grow instead of having the usual period. I think it also stated that this was only to happen to married people.

I don't remember how, but I got wind that my brothers were given a similar booklet for boys so I snooped through the desk drawers in their room one day. I found it, but was afraid of getting caught so I only skimmed the pages quickly. I remember finding the word "masturbation" and looked it up in the dictionary to find the meaning. The definition puzzled me more with the word "orgasm." I looked up "orgasm" but, because I knew nothing about sex, none of it made any sense.

My older sister Bertha gave me a few tips on the period issue as well but my girlfriends and I didn't talk about it too much. We were also discouraged from doing hard physical labor and most girls wouldn't participate in running games at school during their period. During canning season, certain items like cucumbers were canned by someone who wasn't on their period. Mom had a bad experience with all the pickle jars losing their seal and the contents boiling out. The widow next door (Mary) told her it was because she had canned them while on her period so she never took any chances after that.

I think I was ten when my aunt from Indiana, who was several years older than me, told my sister and me that women who get a big belly are going to have a baby. I really knew who was going to have a baby then and not long after that Mom's belly started growing. Secretly I started getting so excited the more obvious it became!

Several times I asked my Mom or sister if we were going to have a baby and they would usually give me the "I have secret" smile and was usually told I wasn't old enough to know. I also noticed my mom stayed home from church or social gatherings, would lie down to rest every day after dinner, and she went to the doctor which was unusual.

One day she came home from the doctor and I went out to carry in groceries. My Dad thought I had gone to the house but I lingered when I heard Dad ask what the doctor said. Mom got embarrassed and I scurried for the house when I got the "this is none of your business look" from Dad. I was observant enough that she gave me little nod and smile one day when I asked and she also told Bertha it was alright to confirm the facts because I knew anyway.

One morning we got up to do the chores and we younger ones were told my parents had gone to the hospital during the night. We all knew what that meant and couldn't wait for Dad to come home with the news. He came home all smiles telling

Winter in early 1996, this cold Iowa day being 30 degrees below zero. When it's cold like this we wear a thick scarf under our bonnets, therefore my head covering is in the bucket I'm carrying.

My family farm just North of Kalona, Iowa.

Using a wagon is typical for hauling certain items, perhaps from neighbor to neighbor.

Three boys at play, dressed in their Sunday clothes.

Mother and daughter shopping in Glasgow, KY. Shopping was a rare and exciting occasion for my siblings and me.

Our summer Sunday School building

Kalona, Iowa.

View toward Kalona from my family farm, North of Kalona, Iowa.

My grandfather's funeral, Kalona, Iowa.

Father and daughter in Mt. Hope, Ohio.

Girls playing "horse and buggy" near Belleville, PA. Notice the "reins" between the "horse and driver"

Two girls near Kalona, Iowa appear to be delivering a note with a message.

Where bicycles are allowed for transportation, women ride them too. Mt. Hope, Ohio.

Swartzentruber Amish girls near Mount Eaton, Ohio.

A softball game at school during recess in Holmes County, Ohio.

Mt. Hope, Ohio.

Stopping at the Smokey Mountains in Gatlinburg, Tennessee while on a trip. I'm the sixth from the left with seven cousins, sister Bertha, and brother Aaron.

Swartzentruber Amish boys at play near Park City, KY.

Harvesting corn, Davies County, IN.

Amish in Pinecraft, Florida, where they don't use buggies.

Women's work is never done.

Taking a break from mowing. Notice the old-fashioned mower because power mowers are not allowed.

Women unloading the hay wagon, families work together during the hay season.

Old Order Amish at an auction in Logsdon Valley, KY.

Young boys help their mother by bringing in the laundry from the clothesline. Ethridge, Tennessee.

us we had a baby boy. I remember jumping up and down and squealing with delight as I ran up and down the stairs, chanting "We have a baby" over and over. I loved babies and it seemed like everyone in our neighborhood was having one.

I was envious but so overjoyed when it was our turn!

"...Guard It Well..."

While Amish culture values the child and supports large families, the challenges and pressures for young people in a closed, patriarchal and scripture-anchored society are immense.

When the social fabric weaves well, the results are remarkably beautiful to see in a young person: a sureness of step, a confidence in one's strength and one's place in the world, an abiding sense of being unconditionally loved and valued, a deep-seated conviction that God's world contains great beauty, and that in living a humble Amish life their salvation is assured.

When things do not go well in the Amish world, the results— particularly for the girls but certainly also for boys— can be tremendously sad: severe physical punishments, verbal assaults, and sexual abuses.

Submission before the church, and humility before God, are key elements in Amish life. The Christian scriptural underpinnings of the Amish church are often employed to support the right of fathers to rule the family, and the boys to have elevated status, thus the design of an Amish community to remain firmly apart from the world of the English and attempt to solve its critical problems from the inside can spell nightmares for Amish girls and women.

If the mother of the family is strong, and the elders of the church are progressive, girls and young women can be helped early to develop a healthy respect for their bodies, to fight against abuse and expect to be protected by the church.

If the mother is not strong, or the elders of the church are conservative and are overly anxious that abuse incidents not embarrass a community, extraordinary efforts can be made to entirely conceal, or at least greatly contain, the news of physical or vicious verbal assault by fathers or brothers against female family members.

A woman beaten by her husband often has no recourse, for submission to her husband and to her church has been the underpinning of all her spiritual training.

A young woman found pregnant by rape is often sent away to another distant community to bear the child, at exactly the time when she would most need the love and support of her mother.

Chastisement of the wife- or child-beater, the molester or the rapist usually comes in the form of spiritual lectures by elders before a church council comprised of other men; punishment can take the form of shunning if the crime is considered unusually vicious. More usual is that the molester or rapist removes himself and his family from that community and settles elsewhere, thus the problem—and the perpetrator—are merely relocated instead of rehabilitated.

County social service units in the largest Amish communities of Pennsylvania, Ohio and Indiana have had for many years specially trained liaisons who work exclusively with the constant stream of young Amish girls and wives who have fled sexual or physical abuse and find themselves on the streets of strange towns or cities without the skills to care for themselves away from the life they have always known.

In those grievous cases which become public knowledge, family social services from the home county in any part of the country will without hesitation intercede by law and remove the girl or teen from the family environment, arrest the perpetrator, and bring the case to court.

The young woman finds no peace even here, for to the Amish mind the English are not saved Christians, and so to remain among the English is to be among the heathen and to accept that Heaven is now out of reach.

All too often, then, the girl begs to be returned to her family and the community asks the aggressor for promises of reform. The perpetrator remains in the community, and the girl must move away to a distant region if she is to have a life unmarked by the community knowledge of her soiling by assault. She is still among the Amish, and therefore once again among the saved.

In recent years the American and Canadian Amish communities have begun to give serious attention to the issues of sexual abuse in their communities. The subject is a matter of discussion among the national gatherings of church elders, and several Amish-authored publications have been printed specifically for distribution to the Amish communities which directly address the need to be watchful for signs of abuse, to encourage children to seek help in need, and to protect the innocent. The booklet *Ignorance is Not Bliss* is a remarkable event in the world of publishing for the Plain People, speaking directly as it does to the tragedy of physical and sexual abuse and the damage done to the child and so to the entire community. *I Wish I Could Have Confided in My Parents* speaks directly to the need for Amish men to see their sweethearts and wives with nothing less than respect and tenderness, to keep the marriage bed a place of loving peace, and to observe only the greatest of care and courtesy in the marriage partnership every day.

"...And God Will Bless You."

Amish girls grow up in the hope that they will be worthy of the promise of Proverbs 31:29:

Many daughters have done virtuously, but thou excellest them all.

To excel in Amish life is to turn one's back on wanting excellence. Individual achievement and ambitious goals are a hope of the English, and can lead only to disharmony and displacement in the community of the church.

So it is that young girls, and the boys too, are taught from their youngest years that their life focus is to be and to do among others: family, neighbors, the church. Without this precept of interdependency, the real meaning of Amish life is lost, and one's very 'Amishness' can be rent like thin cloth. Vigilance, then, for all things cooperative and harmonious, fills the air around the Amish child from first days, and follows the child into the adolescent years to hopefully bloom in the character of the young adult.

The concept of *Gelassenheit*, submission to the authority of the church and scripture, becomes ever more clear as young people grow up. Submission to what is not available—and that will include a great many freedoms that they see around them among their English peers—can also be thoughtfully counter-balanced.

Cooperation paired with creative outlets for young energy and artistic gifts can become essential as the child reaches ado-lescence. Craftwork is always encouraged, and so beautiful baskets, quilts and runners, rocking chairs and bookcases fill the shop shelves, made by hand by young people who are work-ing side-by-side with their parents, older siblings, aunts and uncles, cousins and friends.

As farming is considered the most desirable life for an Amish family, so too are the crafts of the hands considered greatly honorable. Thread, fiber, and wood become elements of art in the crafters' hands, and the labor is done among a community of like-minded companions, perhaps at the kitchen table be-fore a warming woodburning stove, or in a workshop amidst foot-driven machinery and sawdust and sunny windows, or in the peace of a dining-room filled with quilters and frames and quiet conversation.

From these hands come beauty, and every stitch, nail or weave may contain a prayer, for to work with the hands in honorable craft is to praise God. Design for quilt or for basket or chair may come from patterns handed down through many generations of one family, or be shared among families joined by marriage or by church community. The results of this ef-fort is then gladly offered to the outside world, in order that the church community may benefit by their collective labor and realize the return they need to keep members of their community safe and well.

It is natural for young people to want to be helpful, and to have their labors valued, and beyond the life of the immediate family, cooperative work in the larger community becomes an immensely stabilizing force for good for young Amish boys and girls. Caring for the aged or the ill, working as a mother's helper (*maud*), volunteering for frolics such as barn-raisings or other community-wide needs, all turn the young Amish toward the essential philosophy of the Amish church, that it is truly a case of all-for-one and one-for-all, every day, every year, throughout their lives.

By the time Amish young folk reach their later teens, if all has gone well and kindly, they have in the best of times had the opportunity to see the life of peace and mutual support they seek modeled in their parents and in the families around them. They know that they are moving on to the time of religious study, the Dutch College and also to the unique Amish tradition of the *rumspringe* where they can indulge their natural curiosities in greater depth about the outside world.

Beyond? Baptism, the church, and marriage.

CHAPTER EIGHT

Anabaptist

*Therefore go and make disciples of all nations, baptizing
them in the name of the Father and of the Son and of the
Holy Spirit...*
- Matthew 28:19

*A*merica's Amish are *Anabaptist* Christians.

Anabaptists believe that infant baptism is not authorized
by Holy Scripture and should be administered only to pro-
fessed believers who understand what it is that they seek.

Thus, as with other Anabaptist churches such as the Mennonites, Brethren, Hutterites, and the Bruderhof, the Amish
believe that only an informed adult, educated to the true meaning of salvation in Christ, can be accepted into the church by
water baptism.

Blessed are the Peacemakers

For the first Anabaptists fleeing religious persecution in
Central Europe in the middle 1500s, the *Believer's Baptism* was
one of three critical tenets of their faith.

The second tenet was *pacifism*, the refusal to take up arms, and to refuse to obtain or to defend one's rights by force. "...Whomsoever shall smite thee on the right cheek, turn to him the other also." (Matt 5:39) It will fall to all young Anabaptist men to register their beliefs in times of a national draft, and to know that they will be expected to take up some kind of support role in hospitals or service camps that does not require them to use weapons of any kind, or to assist in war.

The third tenet holds that all one's goods are held *in common* with one's brothers and sisters in Christ in accordance with Jesus' teaching that, unless all possessions were given up, there was no hope for salvation (Matt 6:19). Among today's Anabaptist communities only the Hutterites embrace the collective sharing of personal goods: the Amish, Mennonites, and many Brethren churches opt, instead, for as simple or *plain* a life as possible, where personal possessions are minimal and those that are held are without decoration or unnecessary adornment.

So are Anabaptists then also known as the *Plain Peoples*.

If ye know these things, happy are ye if ye do them.
– John 13:17

At the age when young Amish men and women have left grammar school, they are expected to become part of the Dutch College gathering and to begin study for baptism and membership in the Amish church. The several years of learning the High German for Amish church participation, the long and sonorous hymns from the *Ausbund*, and the deeper meaning of the scriptures—particularly as applies to their roles as men and women in community—will eventually resolve in a moment of expressed commitment to the church and a request for baptism. This will most often occur between the ages of sixteen and twenty-one, which is also the accustomed time of the *rumspringe.*

That both can happen simultaneously is one of the unique aspects of Amish life, for the Dutch College can be an arduous spiritual undertaking while the *rumspringe* is a deep dive into the seeming abandonment of Amish life altogether.

The hope is that the young person will see the value of Amish life and, having dipped their toes into the excessive and aggressive ways of the English, will return to their families in contentment, ready to profess their desire to join the church, take up the Amish ways, and to accept baptism in the faith.

The passage known as *rumspringe* occurs in every Amish community but, just as we have seen that Amish communities can differ greatly from each other in style and *Ordnung*, so too can *rumspringe* look wildly different from community to community. The emphasis is on 'wildly!'

In some Old Order communities, *rumspringe* means simply that the boys started to fix up their buggies; girls will experiment with English hairstyles and makeup. (If a girl appears too 'loose' she can get a bad reputation and that will not help her later if she wants to join the church.) *Rumspringe* in my community meant as a church member, a person participated in the young people's group with strict adherence to the *Ordnung.*

Young people are allowed to gather on their own for singings; though it was not permissible for our community, other Amish communities permitted the *junge*—the older teens—to play volleyball together. Boys and girls can date, though it is understood that if a girl says 'yes' to a boy, then it is already pretty serious. If a girl 'serial dates' then, again, she can garner a poor reputation.

In the more conservative communities such as the Swartzentruber, *rumspringe* clothing can mean that the young men really dress up—crisp white shirts, black vests and pants, black broad-brimmed felt hats, black leather driving gloves—and very cool sunglasses! Off they will go, sometimes three or four to an open carriage (their version of a sports car) and driving a classy black thoroughbred, off to where the girls are, usually a Sunday night popcorn and ice cream party. Of course, there is no dancing at Amish parties so it would all look pretty sedate in an Englisher's eyes.

However, in many other Amish communities, *rumspringe* can get pretty wild for the more liberal Amish communities, to the point of dressing in low-cut jeans and t-shirts, fake tattoos and designer athletic shoes. The boys will often cut their hair to English style, leaving behind the classic Amish bangs and bowl cut. The girls may not go so far but they will often wear their hair loose. After all, they have been growing it all their lives and to cut it now would be a major statement of intention to leave. It's enough just to undo the braid, very courageous. Buggies and horses are left behind: many of the boys now own second-hand automobiles which they keep in sheds at the outer edges of the family farm or in a garage in town.

The dance parties can get become quite wild, with rock and hip-hop music on modern entertainment equipment. Parties are often held in the outbuildings of family farms, or in abandoned buildings away from the community, and can be attended by a hundred or more young Amish people who have driven in their cars to get there. The police and county sheriffs in the more liberal communities in Pennsylvania, Ohio and Indiana are very familiar with these gatherings and will intercede if there is evidence of violence or drug-dealing, an increasingly common problem among young Amish people as they try to emulate what they think is popular in English culture.

It is true that some young people now leave Amish life altogether, and try to make their way in the English world. "Try" is the right word here, for they bring very limited schooling in a world that greatly values education, and few saleable work skills beyond carpentry, basic mechanics, sewing and cooking. Their possible employment is in construction, trucking, restaurant work, and the hospitality industry, but they are competing for these entry-wage jobs with many others in the American workforce who can show a high school diploma and a steady work record. For them the world becomes a tremendous challenge, set apart from their families and communities as they must be by the *meidung*, the shunning, and many become exhausted by the struggle and return home again after all.

Despite the supposed allure of English ways, most young Amish passing through rumspringe seem able to work their fascination out of their system at a very high percentage: the numbers gathered by sociologists over the last ten years indicate a very high rate of return by young men and women to Amish life following their passage through *rumspringe*.

It is a statement about the security of a known world, built as it is on cooperative interdependency and the assurance of salvation through works and deeds. The young people are welcomed back into their family life, return to their accustomed roles as children and siblings, don the plain clothing once again, and turn their hearts and minds toward baptism, dating and marriage.

Dating

Just as the level of permissiveness around *rumspringe* can vary greatly, the rules of dating can be very different among Amish communities.

Even the most conservative Amish such as the Swartzentruber allow young men and women who express intention to take baptism and join the church to court within formal and acceptable guidelines, to spend time alone together, and to decide what they want in their future partner. Amish men and women usually marry for love, though there are many times when family disapproval will force a young couple apart, or intense parental pressure may help bring children of neighboring families together. Pregnancy is almost always an automatic precursor to marriage (a shotgun wedding).

Though Amish girls can often hasten the invitation for a date from a boy they admire, it is still the province of the boys to make the first gesture. A girl wants to be very sure about accepting this offer for a date because if she is known to be dating a boy it is hoped that it is serious and the expectations that it will lead to marriage can be very high. Most often young Amish men and women have spent some considerable time looking at each other and visiting amongst each other at the many gatherings held for them around the community. Singing suppers and picnics are very popular opportunities to visit without pressure and to just relax.

If a boy's eye has not fallen on any one particular girl in his home community, he may take the common next step of going to visit—or even to live for a period of time—in the home community of siblings or cousins, or on the farm of his uncles or grandparents. This immerses the young man in a whole new community of dating possibilities and a match-up success may come to him here where it had eluded him at home.

Once a boy and girl agree to date, the courtship rituals are pretty straightforward. He may call upon her with her family's permission, and may visit with her on her front porch (hopefully out of eye and ear of pesky younger siblings), or they may go for a walk or buggy ride in the countryside. Sometimes the dating will take the form of appearing together at a young people's gathering (which in effect declares their togetherness in a culture that promotes secrecy while also craving news and information). Once seen together, it is understood that they have paired off until further notice, and only the immediate families may know of the final outcomes until some time later.

Young Amish people are free to be affectionate toward one another in front of others, though in their very conservative society, such physical affection usually only takes the form of holding hands.

The English are especially curious about the old world customs of *bundling*– or, as it is more commonly known to the Amish, *bed courtship*. It certainly does occur, though the extent of the closeness and the clothing varies greatly from community to community. Also, the more liberal Amish families accept that the young man will enter the family house late at night and go up to the daughter's bedroom where she will receive her young man in her night clothes to pass the hours until dawn, at which time he is expected by the hosting family to be entirely gone from the premises.

Courting in Kalona

I finished school at age fourteen and a year later, I went to German School for six weeks. During this time, girls and boys pretty much keep to themselves but at recess we played games together. It was fun but it lacked the relaxed and familiar atmosphere that existed in grade school.

The boys and girls in most Amish communities mingle more freely than we did in Kalona when the young people get together. Kalona was different, in fact so different that young people visiting from another community once commented that we acted like we were going to bite each other! When we got together, the boys and girls did not mix during the event and there was very little social mingling.

In my home community of Kalona even courting was viewed differently. They had the concept that dating should be taken very seriously almost to the point that you should be willing to marry the person you accept a date with. You were allowed to break up with a person, but dating too many different ones would label you with the image of not being serious about marriage.

Boys were the only ones that could ask for a date. It was

definitely not appropriate for a girl to ask for a date or even act interested in a young man. If she did, she would be labeled as 'boy crazy' and 'desperate.'

The popular girls could show interest and flirt with the boys and not receive the 'label,' but girls behaving in the same manner who were less popular or came from poorer families could receive that label quite quickly.

At the singings we would file into the room with the girls filling every other bench and the boys doing the same. This way the singing sounded great because the harmony was better. We were allowed to sing in parts (unlike in some Amish communities) so our singing sounded wonderful. We would sing for almost two hours, in the first half singing German songs and in the second half singing English songs.

After the singings was when the courting occurred in our community. The boys who had girlfriends would take them home and were allowed to spend a couple of hours with them before returning to their own homes. The couple usually had something to snack on while they visited in a lighted room. They were not to hug, kiss, touch, hold hands, or anything that would lead to sexual contact: that was strictly forbidden.

When a couple was steady, the boy could pick his girlfriend up at her home and take her to the singing as well as taking her home afterwards. They could also date in the same manner during the week only if there was a wedding, a funeral, or some similar important event.

My older brothers followed the standard expectations, and dating began for them after the age of eighteen. Just as with other boys in my community, they would usually ask the girl on a date by getting her brother to ask her, or by writing a letter. Once she consented, they would date every two weeks for a couple months until they wanted to go steady, then they would date every Sunday night.

The couple who started dating would try to keep it a secret as long as possible but it was usually discovered after several weeks. Others that grew suspicious of a new couple would go out of their way to find out if it was true and therefore it became somewhat of a game. Some of the single boys would play pranks on their friends who were dating while they were in the house with their girlfriends.

"...Are Made One With God."

There is a wonderful quote from an Amish bishop of Indiana who spoke pointedly to the proper path in seeking to become a member of the Amish church: "Jesus told us, 'Seek ye first the kingdom of God and his righteousness.' He did *not* say, 'Seek ye first a suitable marriage partner!'"

It is very common for young Amish men and women to request the rites of baptism at the point in time when they know they want to commit to a marriage partner, and so to the larger life of participation in the church community. The penalty for stalling on baptism can be severe: those who seem unwilling to move to baptism can be shunned. Only the baptized may be a member of the church, and the sacrament has an exceptionally solemn meaning, leading inevitably as it does to an avowal to become fully invested in the life of that community and its beliefs. And a fully invested Amish life means marriage and family, and no one may be married within the Amish church unless they have first received baptism.

No matter how a young person comes to ask for baptism, the question is taken up by the church elders and the young person agrees to take instruction in preparation for the sacrament in which they will vow to accept with humility and *gelassenheit* their duties and their place in the community, to wholeheartedly accept Christ as their Lord and accept the church in full fellowship as their hope of salvation.

Unlike many conservative Christian communities, the Amish do not promote the spreading of the Word in the form of proselytizing for conversion. There is acceptance of the beliefs and ways of others but also a deep foundation of belief that to be born Amish is a gift, a blessing. One can pray for the English—all non-Amish—but there is little hope for those lost souls. Thus it is that preaching or witnessing is not a part of this most conservative of Christian communities, but instead there is an avowal to community of faith and belief and a promise to uphold the tenets of a plain life, the *Ordnung*, and the Amish church.

Young people who wish to receive baptism gather for a class of instruction that takes place after the Spring communion, usually from early May through the end of summer. Applicants for baptism will meet with the church's ministers and bishop as a separate class during the every-other Sunday house church meetings where the Dordrecht Confession of Faith is used for instruction in the proper conduct of life in the church.

"Concerning baptism we confess that we penitent believers, who,

through faith, regeneration, and the renewing of the Holy Ghost, are made one with God, and are written in heaven, must, upon such Scriptural confession of faith, and renewing of life, be baptized with water, in the most worthy name of the Father, and of the Son, and of the Holy Ghost..."
- *Article VII of the Dordrecht Confession of Faith*

When the day for baptism is set—usually in the early autumn and before communion—the members of the church are polled for their approval of the applicants who seek fellowship in that church. This is a critical moment in the applicant's path to baptism for the ministers will take great pains to help the young man or woman understand that the path they seek is a difficult one, with little flexibility, and that it would be far less painful for them and for the community of the church to pause and reflect—and withdraw—then go ahead with baptism only to later leave the church.

On the Saturday before the Sunday baptism, the question is put by the bishop to the applicants one last time. Also, the young men are asked to vow that they will accept the role of minister if God should so call upon them by the lot. The girls are asked if they will support their husband should he be called by lot to serve as minister.

On church Sunday, the young people meet one last time with the church elders while the congregation sings hymns, and then they enter the congregation to take their seats on a row of chairs at the front of the gathering. They are wearing clothing special for the occasion: the young women wear the stark garb of black shoes and stockings, black dress and *kapp* with white organdy capes and apron; the boys are similarly dressed in black coat, vest, and pants with a white long-sleeved shirt.

The young men wear a special coat called the *mutza* (mooh'-tzuh) which is traditionally worn by the ministers and the bishop: this signifies a special day for a male member of the church. The black hat is removed before the service begins: men's hats and women's black outer bonnets are always left in an outer room with coats and cloaks.

The ministers enter last, and the singing ceases. The next few hours are filled with sermons and scripture reading.

Finally, the bishop will rise to address each baptism applicant with a final word, and requests them to kneel if they still wish to accept the sacrament as it is based not only on Holy Scripture but also the *Ordnung:*

Do you promise, in the presence of God and His church, with the Lord's help to support these doctrines and regulations, to earnestly fill your place in the church, to help counsel and labor, and not to depart from the same, come what may...?

After their assent to all the baptismal vows and prayers from the German prayer book, the *Christenpflicht,* the bishop, laying his hands on each applicant's head, asks them one last time if they will accept the authority of Christ and the church and live a holy life. Then he says,

"Auf deinen Glauben den du bekennt hast vor Gott und viele Zeugen wirst du getauft in Namen des Vaters, des Sohnes und des Heiligen Geistes, Amen."

(Upon your faith, which you have confessed before God and these many witnesses, you are baptized in the name of the Father, the Son, and the Holy Spirit, Amen.)

Then the deacon dips a small tin cup into the pail of water that he has carried in for this purpose and pours water into the bishop's cupped hands, water which then flows down over the young person's hair and face.

He will do the same with each applicant, baptizing the boys first, then follows his wife down the row of young women where she removes and replaces their *kapps* as each receives the sacraments for baptism.

The young people have remained kneeling until the rite of baptism has been administered to all. The bishop will then reach for the hand of each of the baptized and bid them rise, saying,

"In Name des Herrn und die Gemein, wird die Hand geboten, so steh auf."

(In the name of the Lord and the Church, we extend to you the hand of fellowship, rise up.)

The bishop greets the boys with the Holy Kiss and his wife does the same with the girls, accepting them as new members of the church.

The bishop will speak once again to the assembled congregation, exhorting them to be helpful to the new church members, concluding the sermon with a reading of Romans 6, *"What shall we say then?..."*

The ministers may offer supporting words, and finally the

service is brought to a close where all kneel in prayer to receive a final benediction and to sing a final hymn.

The baptized are now full members of the church, and may participate as adults in all aspects of church life.

I am Baptized

At the time I joined the church, most young people started taking instruction for baptism at age sixteen, but there were some that started at fifteen. Those who waited until they were seventeen or eighteen were viewed as the rebellious ones, the ones who thought the church rules were too much of a burden because they didn't take their salvation seriously enough. I started instructions in the spring after I turned sixteen and was baptized the following August.

There were four girls (including myself) and one boy in my class. We began our series of nine baptism classes by following the ministers to a separate room upstairs from the main church seating rooms, and listened as the bishop read and explained the eighteen articles of faith from the Dordrecht Confession, taking two articles at a time.

In our third class the *Ordnung* of our community was read to us, and we were asked to live by these expectations and apply them to our life. We were told that the community of the church would watch us and that a vote would be taken the Sunday before we were to be baptized to see if they felt our behavior reflected that of one who would be a good and upstanding member of the church.

Though our class was not held back, and we were all subsequently baptized, I have known of many classes which were extended to try to correct the individuals who weren't applying themselves to the *Ordnung* and so could not get a unanimous vote as a class to be baptized. There were also times that, if an individual took too long to comply, he or she was left behind and the rest were baptized. Another attempt could be made by joining a class that began instructions the following year.

After Baptism

Many young Amish people turn earnestly to the question of family and marriage in the year after receiving the sacrament of baptism. Some who have been in serious courtship before taking baptism now go ahead with plans for the wedding. Those who have been only occasionally dating will begin to look more seriously at potential partners in their community and, along with those who have just begun to date, may make plans to remove to another community where extended family are living in order to broaden both the living experience and the potential for suitable partners.

The years in between baptism and marriage can be filled with a variety of experiences available to young Amish adults within the boundaries of social expectations and the *Ordnung*. Both young women and men can become school teachers, though most teachers today are young women, as in the past. Young people may become full partners in a family business, or look for a farm of their own. Some young women hire out as maids in other large households, or go to work in area restaurants and shops that cater to English tourists. Young men may sign on with building crews or become apprentices for a trade with specialists in the Amish community such as the black-smith or harness-maker.

Running as a theme throughout these days is the search for the marriage partner, the husband or wife who will be a match in purpose for the plain life in the Amish world. All paths have been leading to this end.

Amish life is family life, and family life is the very foundation of the Amish church.

CHAPTER NINE

A Price Above Rubies

Who can find a virtuous woman? For her price is far above rubies...
- *Proverbs 31:10*

*I*n the life of the Amish, the sacrament of marriage is second only to that of baptism. Here begins the great cycle of Amish life once again: commitment, birth, growth, and finally death.

It cannot be understated that the partnership of marriage is the primary source of happiness for the individual in Amish life. Here are the fulfillments of body, mind and spirit in a world which greatly circumscribes the vast range of human intellectual, physical, emotional, aesthetic and creative outlets that the English assume for granted in a free society.

For the young woman in Amish society, a great deal will depend on how she was raised by her family, the character of her chosen partner, and the progressive nature of her church. As in all things in Amish life, *gelassenheit*—submission—to her husband and to the *Ordnung* is her only assurance for salvation in a faith which teaches that salvation is found through works and deeds rather than by Grace.

A happy and successful marriage is an event between a husband who understands that his tender and loving care of his wife and children is in perfect balance with her sense of her value, bodily sanctity and freedom of expression within the understood boundaries of the plain life she has chosen. Strong marriages are the rule in Amish life, and to see the unconditional love and support played out between the Amish husband, wife and children—underscored by a great contentment with one's lot and duty—is one of the greatest gifts of the Amish to a hurried and distracted English world.

...Ordained The Same In Paradise...

The Amish, being an agrarian people, have a natural need to tuck their major passages of life into convenient spots in the calendar year. In the instance of birth and death, such planning goes out the window. But in the instance of marriage, a wedding will very definitely be planned in the "down time" of the farm year: late autumn after the harvest is in, or early spring before the planting season begins.

Certain days of the week are designated "wedding days"– Tuesdays and Thursdays– so as not to interfere with critical market days where Amish communities participate in produce auctions and benefits. Saturday weddings are rare because that imitates "English" weddings.

Most Amish weddings will take place in the month of November and there can be a great rush of planning, preparation and travel across the country as family members and friends are notified and invited, for it is the Amish custom to withhold the news of the wedding until the very last moment, often just three weeks before the actual event.

When a couple is ready to get married, the bishop will announce it following a church service before the congregation is dismissed. This is usually done in the bride's church district, and the groom and his family will attend for the occasion.

"...there is in the church of God an honorable state of matrimony, of two free, believing persons, in accordance with the manner after which God originally ordained the same in Paradise..."
- Article XII of the Dordrecht Confession of Faith

Weddings are planned secretly so when the groom and his family come to the bride's district for church, it is usually an indication that the couple will be *ausgerufen* (owz'-geh-roo'-fun) or *published*. The community may suspect an upcoming wedding by telltale signs of the bride's family, such as the painting and tidying up of the farm, much planting of celery in the family garden (a traditional wedding feast food item), new construction to expand the house or erecting an entirely new building in order to accommodate the huge wedding or to prepare a new home for the newlyweds.

The wedding is usually three to four weeks after the couple is published: lengthy engagements are not allowed. During this time the final wedding preparations begin in earnest. The groom starts growing a beard and he stays at the bride's home to help with the preparations.

While the bride and groom are sending handwritten invitations to family and friends, and traveling through their home community to personally invite their guests, family and friends at home that have a part in the wedding help set tables, prepare food, and other necessary preparations.

The wedding is probably the most celebrated occasion for the Amish, where 400 or more guests from near and far are invited to share this special time and the only time that a woman, as a bride, may have her specific preferences realized (to a degree of course). She chooses the decorations of the cake, the color of her wedding dress, the colors of the cooks' and the table-waiters' dresses, and the dishes and other decorations for the *eck*, the special corner table where the wedding party sits after the ceremony. However, flowers, candles, wedding gowns with trains, and fancy tiered wedding cakes, are all considered excessive frills and are not allowed.

The bride and groom choose and couple up enough of their siblings and cousins to have two couples as their attendants (or "witnesses"), sixteen to twenty couples for table-waiters, three or four girls to unwrap and record the gifts, and a couple of girls to take care of the guest books that are passed at each table at meal time. Even young siblings or nieces and nephews get to feel special as gift carriers, taking gifts from the guests as they arrive and carrying them to the gift room.

Occasionally, if the bride's home doesn't have enough room to have the service and feed the guests both, a neighbor may host the service. In this case, three boys called 'hostlers' are assigned to transport the three couples in the wedding party to the bride's home after the ceremony for the festivities.

To be the witnesses for the bride and groom is the highest honor; second highest is the couple (usually close relatives) who are the table-waiters for the *eck*, taking care of the wedding party who have their very own serving bowls and food.

The cooks are usually married siblings and aunts who prepare and dish up the food for the table-waiters to serve. The bishop who marries them is a relative of the bride unless the groom has a closer relative who is a bishop.

The Day of the Wedding

An Amish wedding is an all-day affair and the attendants, table-waiters, and cooks arrive early to begin their long and busy day.

As the guests arrive, the wedding couple and their attendants remain in rooms upstairs, getting dressed and ready for the service. They will dress in all new clothes for this day.

The bride and the two girls in the wedding party dress up like they would for church, in white starched organdy capes and apron instead of those that match the dress and a black head covering. All the other women and girls are wearing "suits" which is a dress with a matching cape and apron and a white head covering. The married women always wear the suits, pinning their cape straight down the front while the unmarried girls pin their capes crossed in the front. Only for church do the unmarried girls wear the white cape and apron with a black head covering.

The wedding service is similar to church except that the songs and sermon reflect the occasion, and the marriage vows are exchanged toward the end of the service as they stand before the bishop.

At 9:00 or 9:30 A.M. the service begins and the ministers file to a room upstairs as they would for church and the couple receives counsel and instructions from them, including what is appropriate when it comes to sex relations in the marriage. (For example, in some Amish communities they are not to have sex till the third night of their married life.)

When the couple leaves the ministers' room they file into the room where the service is, accompanied by their attendants, and sit on the chairs in the front of the ministers' bench. The table-waiters and the girls who unwrap gifts and take care of the guest books all wear a white starched handkerchief pinned to their clothes. The handkerchiefs have a lacy edge and have the names of the bride and groom and the date along with their own names using adhesive letters. The girls pin them to their capes, and also pin the handkerchief to the vest of the boy who is to be their partner for the day.

The table-waiters will file in by couples after their tables are prepared and the cooks as well but only just before the vows are exchanged because they have to keep an eye on the food as it cooks.

The ceremony is much the same as any Sunday service, beginning with the slow and solemn hymns that all Amish church services start with. The main difference will be in the sermons given by the ministers and the bishops: all preaching goes to the nature and sacrament of the marriage in Amish life, supported by appropriate scripture readings drawn from the Old Testament and from the Book of Tobit.

The bride and groom are asked to stand at last. She holds no flowers, nor are there rings to be exchanged: rings would be unseemly, not plain. The bishop asks for their commitment to their intentions, then asks for their vows and, upon assent, all three bend their knees and the bishop blesses them and bids them go forth as husband and wife. The groom does not kiss the bride: such expressions of affection would not be seemly.

The ministers in attendance now give their brief testimony, and often the fathers of the bride and the groom are asked to speak as well. Then the bishop reads the concluding prayers from the *Christenpflicht*, the Amish prayer book, and leads the assembled in a final hymn, concluding the wedding ceremony.

After the vows are exchanged, all the cooks and table-waiters leave the room to go eat and reset the tables for the guests. As the congregation sings the last song, the wedding party files out of the room to a room upstairs where the girls and the bride change their clothing. The girls replace the black head covering for a white one, and the white cape and apron for the colored ones that match their dress. The bride does the same but, because she is now married, she pins her cape straight down the front. As a married woman she will no longer wear the black head covering or the white cape and apron, and will retire them to the closet for safe keeping.

The wedding party sits down at the *eck* and the tables are then filled for the noon meal. A huge meal is served, usually consisting of mashed potatoes, gravy, meat, a vegetable, dressing, sliced cheese, pudding, fruit, cake, pies, and sticks of hard candy.

Each table-waiter couple has a specific table to wait on and, after everyone has eaten, the table-waiters wash all the dishes in preparation for the later evening meal.

After the singing following the noon meal, the bride and groom unwrap some gifts and guests have a chance to greet and wish them well. The afternoon will then pass with much visiting among the community residents and the many visitors until the supper hour.

Supper consists of something like hot ham and cheese sandwiches, chicken and noodles, sliced cheese, perhaps potato salad and a different kind of pudding than for dinner, topped off with ice cream, cake, and strawberries.

The table-waiters will finally eat around 7:00 P.M. and will remain at the table for the singing that begins at 8:00 and ends at 10:45. The rest of the young people are seated on benches like the usual Sunday night singing but, for a wedding, they all have to couple up instead of sitting apart as boys and girls.

This is a fascinating process and always very interesting to see which girl the boy chooses for his partner. The girls all congregate in the yard and a male married member of the family helps get the partnering done. The boys each take a turn to tell him which girl they want as a partner and he will call out her name. This continues until every boy has a partner and there were usually more girls than boys so those that weren't chosen filed in at the end.

Of course, the couples who are dating file in first before the rest of the young people are coupled. Boys try to choose their cousins when possible and I sat with my cousins quite often, although there were times I sat with another boy.

The table-waiters receive a gift from the bride and groom for helping on their special day. These gifts usually are something like a small wooden box, fashioned to hold handkerchiefs or small trinkets. It's almost like a souvenir because it has your name on it along with the bride and groom's name and the date.

I was table-waiter six or seven times for my cousins and also when my brothers Elson and Wilbur got married.

Elson's Wedding

Elson and Loretta were married in March of 1990 and I had turned sixteen not long before.

I was not with the *junge* yet and I wasn't a member of the church although I was taking instructions for baptism. Because I was a sister to the groom, I was asked to be table-waiter: if I hadn't been, I would have had a more modest task such as unwrapping and recording gifts. I was a little afraid I wouldn't fit in with the rest of the table-waiters who were with the *junge* but at the same time I was very excited and felt extra special to have such a special part in Elson's wedding!

Months before the wedding the secret preparations were started. During this time on their dates, Elson and Loretta discussed and planned all the details of the wedding, deciding who would be the cooks, the table-waiters, and so on. Their first task was to personally invite guests to the wedding. They prepared invitations to be mailed to guests once the news of their marriage was "published" or made known, and they also made the handkerchiefs to be pinned to the table-waiters' clothes.

Elson had a new suit tailored and Loretta made her wedding clothes in advance.

The day they were published we went to Loretta's church

district to hear the announcement. I was sad that Elson was leaving home but happy that he was going to live close by. He was going to stay at Loretta's family home to help until the wedding, then they would move to their own farm one mile north of us.

As the groom's family we went to help a great deal in the wedding preparations. I remember setting tables and as the day drew closer we started preparing food, spending one whole day making nothing but angel food cakes!

Elson seemed so happy as he worked next to Loretta when they decorated their *eck* and she had him help make the wedding cake. She was great at decorating cakes so she decorated her own cake. She placed the three-layer tapered cake on a round mirror and decorated it beautifully in white icing. As the wedding couple this is their special time.

On their wedding day we all arrived early. Mom was a cook, Wilbur was table-waiter for the *eck* with his girlfriend and future wife Darla, I was table-waiter with my cousin Cephas, and Bertha and Benedict were in the wedding party as witnesses. Benedict was coupled with Aunt Rosanna and Bertha with Loretta's brother John David. Aaron wasn't old enough to be table-waiter but may have helped unhitch horses for the older guests.

The wedding party and attendants remained upstairs getting dressed and prepared while the guests arrived and the service began. Table-waiters coupled up with their partners to do the tasks assigned them and pinned on their decorative handkerchiefs while Elson and Loretta joined the ministers to receive counsel. The table-waiters and some cooks, especially the mothers of the bride and groom filed out to the shed in time to see the wedding party come in. The rest of the cooks kept an eye on the food but came in to see the vows exchanged.

Elson's suit was dark navy and Loretta's dress was navy blue, as were Bertha's and Rosanna's also, and worn with the white cape and apron and black head covering. The cooks wore navy blue, the table-waiters' dresses were royal blue and the boys wore white shirts with black pants and vest.

My father as minister had the opening sermon and my Grandpa, also as a minister, read the scripture, and Uncle Elmer as bishop married them. Elson looked so strong and handsome next to his beautiful bride: I had always looked up to my big brother.

After the vows were exchanged, we left to eat dinner and reset the tables for the guests. After the service Loretta replaced her white cape and apron for the colored ones that matched her dress, now pinned down the front like a married woman. They took their place behind the *eck* and the rest of the day took on a more festive nature, compared to the solemn and serious wedding ceremony.

I was happy but also anticipated the future when I would become an aunt!

The Married Life

It is very common for newly married couples to settle close to, if not actually on, the farm of one of the newlyweds' parents.

If the wedding has involved an eldest son, he and his new bride will very frequently become the primary tenants on the family farm and full partners in the operation, with the parents moving to the adjacent *dawdy haus*.

If the wedding involves a daughter, the couple will often take up residence in a small building already standing on the property that has been adapted to living quarters, or in one specially built for them before the wedding. It is not uncommon that the sons who have married move to the home community of their brides.

There is no honeymoon for Amish newlyweds as the English would understand it. Sometimes, however, a young couple may be invited to join their parents on a trip shortly after the wedding to establish their married status as a couple.

In some Amish communities, in the first six months after the wedding, the young bride and groom now wearing the badges of their status—he in his growing beard and she in her white *kapp*—may travel about the district and beyond to other communities where friends and relatives live, staying for a few days at each place and collecting the wedding gifts that are waiting for them. The bride has often brought a dowry with her in the form of bedding and quilts, cookware and clothing; many of the larger pieces of furniture and household equipment that are also needed to make an Amish house and home are given at this time by parents, grandparents, and other close relatives.

The bride and groom are also learning their status with each other. The courtship has (hopefully) shown the young people what they might expect in the balance of their marriage, but it is the first year in married life, living within the *Ordnung*, that will set the marriage on a healthy or less easy track.

The questions of authority and power of decision-making

become primary now. The exhortation of Ephesians 5:22-23 is a powerful underpinning of Amish life: "Wives, submit yourselves unto your own husbands, as unto the Lord. For the husband is the head of the wife, even as Christ is the head of the church."

How coldly, or kindly, the new young husband observes this basic tenet of the Amish church will set the course for the nature of the marriage, and the happiness of the bride, in the years to follow.

There will be other pressures: for the young bride, her household becomes her entire world. Where her husband may continue to partner with father and brothers to work a farm, she alone is responsible for the home and is very much on her own, at least until such time as her young children have grown old enough to be of real help to her. And children come early and often in Amish families: the young people will have (God willing) very little time to catch their breath as they return from their honeymoon of travel and begin in earnest to live their new lives—and their new family.

Happiness comes, the newlyweds are taught, from submission to God, the church, and the *Ordnung*.

Those who can embrace the command of *gelassenheit* do well in this life.

Those whose natural creative, or intellectual, or spiritual drive leads them to ask questions—or to crave experience outside of the confines of the Amish world—often fare less well.

This can lead to conflict, and to anguish, and to hard choices: for the individual, for their children, for their church.

CHAPTER TEN

Hard Choices

Likewise...submit yourselves unto the elders. Yea, all of you be subject to one another.
- I Peter 5:5

My paternal Grandfather, Tobias J. Miller, died in 1996 in Kalona at the age of 83. I was 22 years old at the time, baptized and a member of the church.

Grandpa was a minister of long standing, and the patriarch of a dynasty of ten Miller sons who came to dominate the Kalona Old Order Amish community in an extraordinary way. Grandpa was the unchallenged power in our community and a national figure among the Amish in the United States. We knew the funeral would have an enormous attendance.

Immediately after his passing, friends and neighbors arrived to clean and prepare the house for the funeral which would occur three days later. Grandpa's family also asked the Washington County Sheriff's office to contact their colleagues in other counties in Iowa and in other states around the country to let relatives and friends know of Grandpa's death.

After his body was prepared by the local funeral home (as required by Iowa law), he was placed in a plain white linen-lined casket made by a local Amish man, dressed in his Sunday suit (men are always dressed in their black Sunday dress for burial), and the open casket was placed on sawhorses in his bedroom at home.

Food was brought in to feed the family and the many arriving visitors, and neighbors came to help with the chores while people arrived to view the body and comfort the family.

During those three days my parents spent most of the time at Grandpa's house, but we children only went for the wake and one afternoon prior to the funeral. We had to do the farm chores while my parents were gone.

Grandpa's funeral was like any other but, because he was so well known, his funeral was very large and vanloads of Amish were soon coming in from around the country, most arriving the day before the funeral. The night before the funeral was the wake, and all the young people of the community gathered for almost two hours to sing German and English hymns for the occasion. After the singing, all of them filed past the casket to view the body as did many others that had come for the wake.

The family sat together during the funeral while the rest of the congregation sat as they would for church. Grandpa's sons and their wives sat up front closest to the casket and I sat with my siblings and the rest of the grandchildren behind our parents.

All the women and girls wore black and the women in the immediate family continued to wearing black on Sundays for quite sometime after the funeral. As a grandchild, I would wear black for six months and my mom as a daughter-in-law would wear black for a year. (The more distant the relative the less time you wore black following the funeral.)

Preaching was done by a minister in his district or a visiting minister. The officiating was done by the bishop in Grandpa's district. There was no singing but the rest of the service was somewhat like a church service. The preaching and prayers were structured to comfort the grieving but also to admonish and warn the congregation to be ready for death because it is so final.

After the preaching a poem was read and then the obituary was read. Everyone filed past the casket to view the body and then the immediate family gathered around the casket to weep and view the body for the last time.

The casket was closed and the six pallbearers, men from his church district, carried it to the waiting coffin buggy. The family got into their own waiting buggies (already thoughtfully hitched up by neighbors) and followed the casket to the cemetery where the pallbearers had prepared a grave, accompanied mostly by close family.

The bishop spoke and offered a prayer and young people in his church district sang while the pallbearers buried the body. The immediate family stood the closest to the grave to watch and weep. There were no flowers at the funeral, as is usual among the Amish, nor was the grave adorned with flowers.

While we were at the cemetery, people from Grandpa's church district were back at the farmhouse feeding visitors from out-of-state. When the family returned, they were seated at tables and the rest of the people were fed as the women handed them trays filled with food that was brought in. As with Amish weddings, many hands made light work of the serving and the cleaning up, leaving the immediate family to rest and visit quietly with friends and relatives.

Out-of-town guests usually stayed overnight at the houses of church members in the district, took breakfast with the family in the morning, and went home again.

Lake of Fire

Death by illness and accident comes more often to the Amish than to the greater American population by virtue of a hard, unmechanized agrarian existence and—though certainly willing to seek modern medical care in an emergency—they have an abiding faith in natural medicine for the cure of most bodily ills.

As the sacraments of baptism and marriage are based upon merit by works and deeds, so is death seen to be the final judgment call on a life of merit, or demerit.

The Amish view death as a stark ending to one's life, its value to now be wholly at the mercy of God's judgment. The deceased will now stand at the Judgment Seat of God as the Book of Life is opened, and one has to give account for everything they have done during their life on earth, good or bad.

The Amish believe that you should be prepared at all times because you never know when your time will come and there are no second chances after death. They believe that one should live a life in accord with God's expectations as set forth by scripture and the *Ordnung* in order to have eternal life in Heaven, or else your soul will suffer eternal punishment as it is cast into outer darkness, into the everlasting Lake of Fire.

And cast ye the unprofitable servant into outer darkness,
where there is weeping and gnashing of teeth...
- Matt 25:30

This is preached regularly in church and to the children to help them accept right from wrong, promote obedience to parents, to do good, get baptized, join the church and be a good upstanding member of the church if we want to go to Heaven when we die. The pressure, obviously, is enormous and can consume the very being of an Amish individual in an abiding fear for their souls.

Though the Amish do not believe they have the right to judge someone who dies, they also don't believe there is much hope for a young person who dies rebellious or who has refused to join the church.

They have *no* hope for someone who has been excommunicated, or who dies in the ban (shunned), nor for someone who commits suicide. It is not unheard of in some Amish communities that individuals who had committed suicide or died in the ban were not buried with their family but instead were buried in a fenced-off corner or outside the cemetery altogether, away from hallowed ground.

Better it is to be a humble spirit with the lowly,
Than to divide the spoil with the proud.
- Prov 16:19

The burden of the spirit, for an individual who strives to live happily in the midst of a people whose very salvation is predicated upon works and deeds, can be grievous. So it was for me.

I was troubled shortly after I took my place as a member of my church community, following my baptism at the age of 16. I was unprepared for the natural clashes of human nature among a people who, by virtue of the cultural, social and religious rules, needed to keep a close watch on each other so as not to let one lamb stray from the path to God. I was unprepared to face the real narrowness of generosity that was often displayed, nor could I easily reconcile such close-heartedness with the often startling drive for power and status that was demonstrated, for such drive was not manifested through material goods or property but rather through the highly visible and public disdain for the same.

"Love not the world, neither the things that are in the world." (I John 2:15). It is never possible to be too *good* in Amish life. Even a culture of plainness can have its divas, and tale-telling to the ministers and to the bishop was more than just acceptable, it was expected, and so one could be brought up before the gathered community of the church on a Sunday morning to explain a shortened hemline, a smaller hat brim, or too frequent use of a neighbor's telephone. One could and did easily bring shame upon themselves and upon their families if they appeared to be straying too far from the rules of the *Ordnung*, or failed to show proper *gelassenheit*.

Sometimes too, the *Ordnung* was applied— or *not* applied— with maddening inconsistency. There was a rule in the Kalona church *Ordnung* about the use of tractors, stating that after the purchase of a tractor, steel wheels must replace the rubber ones so that the tractor can never be used on the county roads but only in the fields and farm lane back to the barn. The rubber wheels are not to be put back on the tractor for use, but only for resale. Any transgression of this rule in the *Ordnung* meant confession before taking communion.

Young men in our community played more than a bit with this particular rule, buying a tractor right after communion and using it with the rubber wheels. Amish have communion twice a year and because one can occasionally skip communion once without too much trouble, they didn't bother getting their tractor in order, knowing that they would not be taking communion. This way they could use the rubber-tire tractor for a full year, and everyone looked the other way whenever it happened. My brother Elson's brother-in-law would routinely use his tractor like a car running back and forth to town, and he lived right next to the bishop!

During this time, Elson put his own tractor up for sale and so needed to put the rubber wheels back on it. He had bought a hog shed at an auction and had decided to use the tractor just that once instead of hiring someone to get it.

For this one transgression, they asked Elson–my dear brother who meant no harm–to make a confession in church! It happened that this was the first time I had witnessed the confessions after becoming a member of the church, and I was appalled and secretly very upset how unfair it was that they singled Elson out to be an example. It seemed so wrong and it really opened my eyes of how inconsistently legalistic it all was.

There is no question that the Amish—family, friends, neighbors, and community—always help each other out to build and to harvest, or during funerals or for any misfortunes that may befall someone in the Amish community. This is a wonderful trait, and is the one that causes real wistfulness in the English who have come to admire the Amish life of plainness and interdependency and the real beauty of community character that such a life can display. It is all true, all of it.

The downside to being a close-knit community is that there is little room for individuality. You have to blend in and be like everyone else and everyone watches one another and reports infractions of the *Ordnung* to the bishop or ministers in order to keep everyone in line. One is expected to tell if they have witnessed a misdeed because, if they don't, they are considered to be as much at fault as the one who did it.

Because of the strict boundaries set forth for everyone to follow, this creates a lot of bickering and fault-finding within the church when some follow the rules more closely than others. It is undisputed that this type of environment too often fosters prejudices and intolerance of others' weaknesses simply in order to save one's own soul.

There is a particularly damaging element of *power struggle* in any Amish community—humans are humans, after all—and the ones with the most power are the bishops, and ministers fall next in line. Some men who want power and control, yearn and strive to become a bishop, often moving to other church districts in their community, or to other Amish communities altogether to improve the chance that the lot will fall to them the next time a bishop is to be elected out of the group of ministers in the district.

My dad and his younger brother Elmer became ministers by lot in the same year of 1971. The following year Elmer became bishop, thus being the bishop of our church district ever since.

My grandfather was a minister in a different church district, but some local English people thought he was not only his church district's bishop but possibly the *head* bishop. There is no such thing as a "head bishop" in the Amish church. He was just a powerful and well-known man in his own community and in other Amish communities around the country, frequently traveling to be part of regional meetings and to make his voice heard.

He was also a very shrewd man, owning a tremendous amount of valuable real estate in and around Kalona, and loaning poorer bishops and ministers money, knowing very well that they couldn't pay it back. In return, they owed him "favors" and he would call them with deft timing. He became a very wealthy man in his later years, what the English would call "upper middle class" in income and savings, yet he lived about as plainly as any other folks in our community at Kalona. Ostentatiousness was not his thing. His wealth was in his power, and he used it.

Because he had power, I do not believe that he was called to confession or asked to defend his ways. So it is in many, many Amish communities. A family that finds itself unhappy with such a state of affairs in the community may move several times in the attempt to find an Amish community in better balance with itself.

Hard Choices

I now worked at home most of the time, but at the age of seventeen my first niece, Elnora, was born to Elson and Loretta. I was their *maud* (child-care helper) for six weeks and served in the same role for their next two children.

I was twenty-one and teaching school when their fourth child was born and even though I loved my school teaching job, I longed to be at Elson's. My eldest brother and I had grown even closer, Loretta had become like my sister, and I loved the children like my own. There was so much love and happiness and today they are a happy family of ten.

I don't know if I would have left the Amish had Ottie, an Englisher who later became my husband, not come along. That I will never know, but I do know I was growing extremely unhappy.

Elson's confession, the inconsistencies of the rules not applying to everyone the same, scrutiny of one another, and the discord and bickering of what should and shouldn't be allowed, were wearing on my mind and keeping a shadow over my heart.

I kept my doubts about the church to myself for fear I would be watched closely if they thought I was dissatisfied enough to leave. Along with that, my dad was getting more and more intolerable with verbal abuse and moodiness. He had always been very hard on my mother and on us children but as I grew into womanhood I was torn between the Amish ideal of a kind and loving head of the household, and the reality of my father's behavior. My brother Elson was not at all like him, so I had a wonderful example of what an Amish man could be, but I was

A family with twins in Kalona, Iowa.

A family at work in Ohio. Notice the hand-made tool being used to make multiple furrows for planting the garden.

Haymaking time for this family near Horse Cave, KY.

Church service held in a barn, kneeling in prayer.

In Park City, Kentucky, Swartzentruber Amish women hired by an "English" neighbor plant tobacco. These Amish grow and use tobacco themselves.

First day of a new school year. Glasgow, KY.

*Standing with my cousins, brother, and sister on a mountaintop in Virginia.
I'm the fifth from the left.*

This is an Amish family auction. Only family members are invited to attend.

Roadside vegetable stand in Glasgow, Kentucky.

Girls' day out

Family outing, Horse Cave, Kentucky.

Bringing in a load of hay in Rebersburg, PA. Notice the mule on the left. Most Amish won't use mules but the Amish in Pennsylvania do.

A young girl caring for her younger brothers in Charm, Ohio.

Amish girls in Pinecraft, Florida.

Amish at a bus station in Kidron, Ohio.

This is most likely a funeral service because all the women are wearing black. Annabel, Missouri.

Western Pennsylvania.

Amish in Pinecraft, Florida.

Headed for school, Glasgow, KY.

Gathered for an evening chat. Lancaster, PA.

This is the bonnet I used to wear, depicting the style of Old Order Amish in Kalona, Iowa.

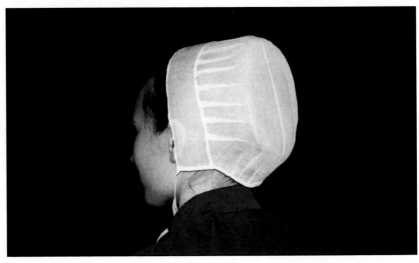

A head covering or kapp *of Kalona, Iowa, the one I used to wear.*

A head covering typically worn by the Old Order Amish in Lancaster, Pennsylvania. Notice how it's almost heart shaped, the most distinctive style of Amish head coverings.

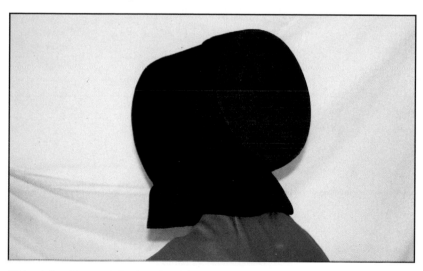

This style of bonnet depicts the Old Order Amish in Holmes County and other parts of Ohio. Old Order Amish in different parts of Indiana use a similar bonnet.

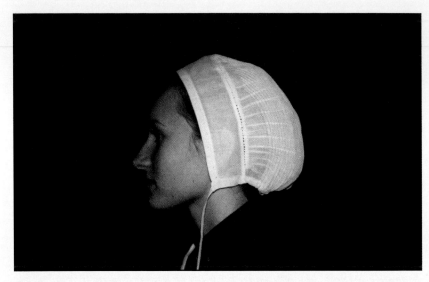

A typical Swartzentruber Amish head covering.

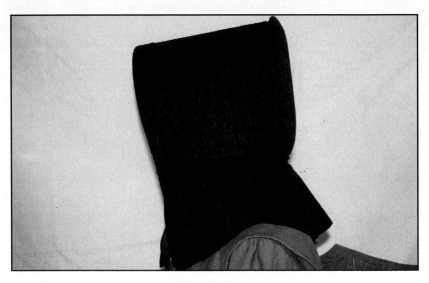

A Swartzentruber Amish bonnet.

seeing too few of this same example around me in my community to have real hope.

As my anguish grew, and I contemplated my options, I did first consider leaving to join the neighboring Mennonites in the Kalona area, a more liberal—but still plain—Anabaptist community. This would mean that I would make my family and my church community unhappy but at least I would not be excommunicated or shunned.

There were quite a few different types of Mennonites around my community with different degrees of strictness. The most conservative were groups known as Old Order Mennonites: they usually still used horses, but they would permit telephones and electricity in the house. Though Old Order Mennonites can be found in many parts of Iowa and the Upper Midwest, there were no close settlements anywhere near Kalona so that was not an option for me.

There were Beachy Mennonites and several other groups similar to them such as Haven, Salem, and Sharon Bethal Mennonites in the Kalona area. But these groups were far more liberal, and they all owned automobiles. Then there was the Fairview Church: these Mennonites called themselves "conservative" but they were just a notch under the Kalona Mennonites who were very liberal and dressed just like Englishers.

The Kalona Amish got along well enough with the different Mennonite groups and would hire them as drivers as long as they weren't going to a strict Amish community. Mennonite drivers who were former Amish would actually be shunned by these stricter communities; English drivers were preferable and would be hired instead.

Even though the Amish and the Mennonites existed together in the Kalona area, it was frowned upon for our worlds to cross too much. It was unacceptable to the Amish for their members to attend Mennonite churches for fellowship: that could lead to the desire to join the more liberal church.

Unlike my own Old Order Amish community at Kalona, very strict settlements like the Swartzentruber Amish will excommunicate fellow members of their church should they leave to join a Mennonite church; the Amish sorely dislike losing members.

"...Warn the Wicked of His Way..."

I did not go to the Mennonites. I went to Ottie Garrett. Ottie, a happy, laughing, brilliant, gifted, tender, greathearted man. And an Englisher. Our family had known him for years: he often drove for my grandfather and my uncles in Kalona in his big, specially outfitted van, taking any and all of us around the county, around the state, around the country.

I had fallen in love with someone who was kind, loving, and possessed a carefree happiness that I wanted to be a part of. I couldn't bear to hurt my mother, or my nieces and nephews who were so dear to me. I feared for the children the most because I was afraid they wouldn't understand and be angry with me because of the image given by the Amish. But I wanted so much to be with the one I loved and was happy with. I cried and prayed many a night for guidance.

We knew each other many years before we spoke to what had been true for some time: We loved each other, we wanted to marry, and I would have to leave my home.

I made my decision one morning and, after years of sadness and anguish, I was gone.

And I was shunned. The *meidung*, the shunning, to be put in the ban.

It has been many years now, and the sense of utter separation has abated, but its impact has not lessened.

"...if thou warn the wicked of his way to turn from it: if he does not turn from his way, he shall die in his iniquity."
- Ezekiel 33:9

It is the ultimate statement from the Amish. Would my soul be in peril? For the Amish truly believe that those who leave the church are doomed, as the English already are. I balanced on a knife-edge, needing to leave but sure that my salvation was lost. I knew it would not just be from my own family and my own community of Kalona but from other Amish folk as well: the news followed me to Kentucky where I have made my home with Ottie, and even here some of our Amish neighbors still will not exchange pleasantries in passing or do any business with me.

I understand the price I have paid for my choice and, as other young people who have needed to leave their Amish lives find their way in the night to our front door, clutching children and what small possessions they could carry away, I do my utmost to help them understand the full meaning of the path they have chosen. Some go home again, most make their way into English society.

I have made a new life, a new family, and have found my own work at Ottie's side. Together we write, we speak and we travel to wherever we are asked, to tell my story once again and share with new friends the beauties and challenges of the life I came from.

And though English life will never quite offer the interdependency of the Amish as they work for and around each other to accomplish common goals, the bigger world is filled with loving and generous people wherever I look for them, as is *always* true in God's family.

My choice was not the common choice for the Amish, but it was right for me. Yes, absolutely, I miss the warmth of my family, the daily life on the farm, and my community at Kalona.

Even so, I am happy in my new life, and my soul is at peace for I have found that salvation is promised us not in works and deeds but in God's sure Grace.

I am no longer lost, but found.

The Wings of the Morning

$\mathcal{N}$ow after leaving the Amish I look back with a perspective I never had before.

I am happy and free, like a bird from its cage, free from bondage. In spite of the heartache, tears, and turmoil of losing my family because of my decision, I am happy and at peace. I miss the family I used to know and that I was once a part of, but many things of my old life I still practice, like gardening, canning, cooking, and such.

Today, as a published author and lecturer, I enjoy sharing the joy and happiness of my faith and my experience.

By no means do I regret growing up Amish, but rather cherish the experience and perspective it has given me.

My future looks bright, and I hope to have a family. I have my G.E.D. now and I know that I will one day go to college, too. Me! An Amish girl, winner of so many spelling bees, grade schoolteacher...in college! It's a dream I have.

Together, Ottie and I have a wonderful, love-filled life. His kindness and respect, support and wonderful cheer make every day a day worth looking forward to.

I am a member of a fine Lutheran congregation in Bowling

Green.   They have been my rock and my true foundation since the day I first came to worship there. They understand me, and I love them.

Through a journey of faith and grace I've discovered God not to be a punitive God, but God who is loving and forgiving.

My soul's salvation is not based on works and deeds but on Grace, and only on Grace.

Blessed be His Name.

Ruth Irene Garrett

Whither shall I go from Thy Spirit?
Whither shall I flee from Your presence?
If I ascend up into heaven, Thou art there.
If I make my bed in Hell, behold! Thou art there.
If I take the wings of the morning,
 and dwell in the uttermost parts of the sea,
Even there shall Thy hand lead me,
And Thy right hand shall hold me.
If I say, Surely the darkness shall cover me,
Even the night shall be light about me.
Yes, though the darkness hideth not from Thee
But the night shineth as the day:
The darkness and light are both alike to Thee.
                                    - Psalms 139:7-12

Further Resources & Reading

Visiting the Amish Community at Kalona:

Kalona Area Chamber of Commerce
514 'B' Avenue
Kalona, IA 52247
319-656-2660
chamber@kctc.net
http://www.kalonachamber.org/

Kalona Annual Quilt Show & Sale
April 2004
319-656-4489
kac@kctc.net

Kalona Draft Horse Sales
Spring Draft Horse Sale – March 2004
Fall Draft Horse Sale - October 2004
319-656-2222

Kalona Historical Village
Iowa Mennonite Museum & Archives
715 'D' Ave.
P.O. Box 292
Kalona IA   52247
319-656-2519
info@kalonaiowa.org
http://www.kalonaiowa.org/village/

Recommended Internet Resources on Amish Life:

Mennonite Information Center, Lancaster County PA
(An excellent general resource on Mennonite and Amish life)
> http://mennoniteinfoctr.tripod.com/

Amish Heartland On-Line
(An excellent general resource on Amish culture)
http://www.amish-heartland.com/

Amish.Net
(Focuses exclusively on the Amish of Pennsylvania, Ohio and
Indiana)
http://www.amish.net

The Amish of the Bluff Country
(Focuses exclusively on the Amish of the Upper Midwest)
http://www.regionalresearch.net/pages/amish_main.html

ReligiousTolerance.org
(An outstanding resource for study of Amish religious
    historyand beliefs)
http://www.religioustolerance.org/amish.htm

Berks County Webquest
(A very good study unit resource for students grades 6-12)
http://www.berksiu.k12.pa.us/webquest/wandell/index.htm

Fenn Elementary School Amish Links
(A very good compilation of articles for students grades 6-12)
http://www.mcsoh.org/fenn/social_studies1.htm

Suggested readings on Upper Midwest Amish life:

The Amish in Wisconsin. Richard Lee Dawley. Amish Insight,
    2003.

The Amish of Harmony. Drucilla Milne. Rochester, MN: Davies
    Printing, 1993.

*The Amish on the Iowa Prairie: Recreating Community and Iden-
    tity, 1840-1910.* Steven D. Reschly. Center Books in
    Anabaptist Studies: Johns Hopkins University Press, 2000

Amish Roots: A Treasury of History, Wisdom, and Lore. John A.
    Hostetler.
Center Books in Anabaptist Studies: Johns Hopkins Univer-
    sity Press, 1989

Growing Up Amish. Richard Ammon. Atheneum Books, 1989.

A Guide to the Amish of the Bluff Country: Iowa, Minnesota, Wisconsin. Deborah Morse-Kahn. Prairie Smoke Press, 2004

On the Backroad to Heaven: Old Order Hutterites, Mennonites, Amish, and Brethren. Donald B. Kraybill and Carl F. Bowman. Center Books in Anabaptist Studies: Johns Hopkins University Press, 2001.

Plain and Simple: A Woman's Journey to the Amish. Sue Bender. HarperSanFrancisco, 1989.

A Quiet and Peaceable Life. John L. Ruth. People's Place Book No. 2: Good Books, 1997 [1979].

A Quiet Moment in Time: A Contemporary View of Amish Society. George M. Kreps, Joseph F. Donnermeyer, and Marty W. Krebs. Carlisle Press, 1997.

Sarah' Seasons: An Amish Diary and Conversation. Martha Moore Davis. University of Iowa Press, 1997.

Visits With the Amish: Impressions of the Plain Life. Linda Egenes. Iowa State Press, 2000.

Suggested films on Amish life:
(Available through libraries, Amazon.com and other retail video
   vendors)

Amish: A People of Preservation
Vision Video, 1992

Amish Values & Virtues
Tapeworm Films, 1999

Amish-Not to Be Modern
MPI Home Video, 1994

Reflections of Amish Life
Tapeworm Films, 1999

The Amish and Us
Direct Cinema Limited, 1998

Amish Barn Raising
Tapeworm Films, 1999

If you enjoyed *Born Amish,* there's more from **Ruth Irene Garrett**

The Pictorial Companion to *Born Amish,* this luxurious coffee-table book features hundreds of stunning, full-color photos from Amish communities across America, including Ruth Irene's Home and Community, providing an inside look at Amish life never seen by outsiders. Chapters are: Irene, Scenery, Buggies, Quilts, Agriculture and Animals, School Children, Farms, Adults and unusual scenes.

Order your copy today! Only $29.95

(+ shipping and handling) Call Turner Publishing Company

1-800-788-3350   P.O. box 3101,
Paducah, KY., 42002

Also available...

A CD Sampler of Amish Music. Hear Ruth Irene and friends sing authentic, Amish hymns in German, but with a new twist!

FREE! (please include $3.00 shipping and handling.)
Send check or Money Order to :

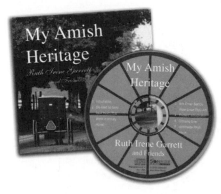

Sonrise Records
171 County Hwy. 430
Oran, MO 63771

Index